Incredible
VISUAL
illusions

Incredible
VISUAL
illusions

Al Seckel

ILLUSION WORKS

Capella

This volume is dedicated to:

Magician Jerry Andrus, a creative genius with optical illusions, and who first inspired my love of optical illusions.

Professor L. Pearce Williams, my former mentor, who taught me the value of excellence.

Physicist Richard Feynman, who gave me a tremendous box of tools, and who showed me how much fun it was to find things out.

Neuroscientist Christof Koch, who has given me so much support and encouragement in my work.

Mathematical games columnist and author Martin Gardner, who served as my intellectual hero in my youth, and who later was so generous with his time and files.

A.S.

Acknowledgements:

Jerry Andrus, Ted Adelson, Stuart Anstis, Irving Biederman, Joe Bogan, Patrick Cavanagh, Jos De Mey, Sandro Del Prete, Jerry Downs, Shigeo Fukuda, Martin Gardner, Richard Gregory, Donald Hoffmann, Keith Kay, Akiyoshi Kitaoka, Alice Klarke, Ken Knowlton, Christof Koch, Scot Morris, Istvan Orosz, Baingio Pinna, Dale Purves, Vilaymur Ramachandran, Tim Rowett, Pawan Sinha, Shin Shimojo, Dejan Todorovic, Walter Wick, Carol Yin.

This edition published in 2007 by Arcturus Publishing Limited
26/27 Bickels Yard, 151–153 Bermondsey Street,
London SE1 3HA

ISBN: 978-1-84193-197-5

Edited by Rebecca Panayiotou and Tessa Rose
Cover design by Alex Ingr
Text design by Christopher Smith

Printed in Singapore

CONTENTS

*M*ost of us take vision for granted. After all, it comes to us so easily. With normal vision we are able to navigate quickly and efficiently through a visually rich three-dimensional world of light, shading, texture, and colour – a complex world in motion, with objects of different sizes at differing distances. Looking about gives us a definite sense of the 'real world'.

In fact, our visual system is so successful at building an accurate representation of the real world through perception that most of us do not realize what a difficult task our brain is performing. Without conscious thought, our visual system gathers and interprets complex information, providing us with a seamless personal view of our environment. The complexities of how we perceive are cleverly concealed by a successful visual system.

Many scientists have underestimated how difficult it is to solve the problem of perception. For example, as recently as the late 1970s and early 1980s, various leaders in the artificial intelligence community, who were concerned with machine learning, boasted that the task to build a computer that would perceive objects would be a simple and achievable goal. On the other hand, building a computer that would consistently beat the world chess master in a game of chess would be incredibly difficult, and as such was for many years the Holy Grail of AI researchers. Years later, it turned out to be just the opposite! Building a computer that could beat the world chess champion in a game of chess turned out to be relatively straightforward. Building a computer to recognize, much less perceive, even the simplest objects has turned out to be incredibly difficult. Those working on the problem have made little progress.

It is sometimes difficult for us to appreciate the problem of vision, because our perception is of a seamless representation of the real world. It might seem reasonable for us to assume that your visual system 'sees' the retinal image in much the way that a digital camera records what it 'sees'. Although it seems like a useful analogy, there is no real comparison between our visual system and a camera beyond a strictly surface level. This is because the camera records incoming information, but your brain interprets incoming information. Your brain is the great interpreter. Furthermore, it feels to us as if a photograph reproduces a three-dimensional world, but it doesn't. It only suggests one. The same visual system that interprets the world around us also interprets the photograph to make it appear as a three-dimensional scene. As you will see throughout this book, your brain is constantly interpreting visual information to create your perception.

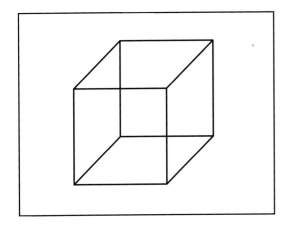

A Necker cube. Fixate on this and it will reverse in depth.

Your perception is not always perfect. Sometimes your brain will interpret a static image on the retina in more than one way. A skeleton cube, known as a Necker cube, is a classic example of a single image that is interpreted in more than one way. If you fixate on this cube for any length of time, it will spontaneously reverse in depth, even though the image on your retina remains constant. Your brain interprets this image differently because of conflicting depth cues.

Most of us don't normally notice the difficulties associated with vision, because our brain automatically resolves them for us. Let us look at just a few examples.

Take a moment to look at the world around you. Move your eyes around the room. Tilt your head. The world stays stable. Imagine what would happen if you watched a movie filmed by a toddler who moved the camera in an irregular manner. You would get positively ill! Your brain somehow stabilizes the images that you see in a way that is coordinated with both your eye and head movements.

Look at some object – a chair close by, for example. Walk around the chair as you look at it. It can even be partially occluded. The chair's image on your retina changes in shape, size, and illumination, yet you perceive it throughout as being the same chair. There is constancy to your perception of objects. This is an aspect of perception most of us take very much for granted. In contrast, people who have suddenly been given sight, after being blind for many years, have various difficulties in interpreting our world.

Another example that we normally do not think about is blinking. Normal blinking occurs about once every four seconds without any external stimulus; it is initiated by signals from the brain. It takes about a third of a second from the beginning of a blink, when the lids first begin to move, until they return to their resting point. For about half of this time, the eyelids are completely closed, reducing the amount of light reaching the retina by around 90 percent. But if you are standing in a lighted room, and an external light is turned on and off for this same length of time, a brief blackout is very noticeable. So, why do we not notice our blinks? How does our visual system fill in the blinked-out period with a seamless visual sensation?

It is well known that having two eyes allows us to have depth perception. However, if you close one of your eyes, you do not immediately lose depth perception. Why not?

7

Finally, think about the formation of the image on the back of your retina. It is very much like the image in a pinhole camera – the image is inverted and switched left for right. Yet, we perceive a world that is upright and properly oriented. How does the brain do this?

These are only a few examples of problems our brains solve every moment we're visually active. Yet, these are not even necessarily the questions that make understanding visual perception so difficult. Far more astounding is our brain's ability to represent reality accurately using the ambiguous information presented by the world.

The great German physicist and physiologist Hermann von Helmholtz first discovered the basic problem of perception over one hundred years ago. He correctly reasoned that the visual information from our world that is projected onto the back of the retina is spatially ambiguous.

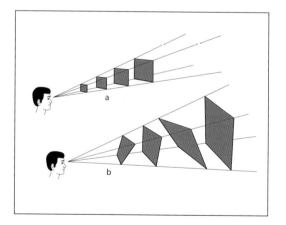

Retinal information about shape is inherently ambiguous.

*This can be illustrated in the following way. Look at the figure on the left.
All the objects subtend the same visual angle to the eye, and have corresponding corners along the same lines of sight, as shown by the long lines converging near the observer's eye. This means that there can be an infinite variety of shapes that can give rise to the same retinal image, as long as they subtend the same visual angle to the eye.*

Fukuda's Strange Piano.

The ambiguity of spatial information can be seen in its extreme in the distorted piano illusion created by Japanese artist Shigeo Fukuda. If you are standing at a fixed viewpoint, the disorganized mess of piano parts on the right will cast a reflection of a perfect piano in the mirror on the left. Standing from this fixed viewpoint, all the physical parts of the piano subtend the same visual angle to the eye as a real piano. When seen from any other angle, they do not, and hence you see their true configuration.

However, the concept of visual ambiguity is far deeper than what Helmholtz originally proposed, because it turns out that any one aspect of visual information, not just spatial, could have arisen from infinitely many different conditions. It is very hard to appreciate this fact at first, because what we perceive in a normal viewing environment is not at all ambiguous.

If all visual stimuli are inherently ambiguous, how does the visual/perceptual system discard the infinite variety of possible conditions to settle on the correct interpretation almost all the time, and in such a quick and efficient manner? This is known in vision science as the 'inverse problem'. Put very simply, the problem is: how does the visual system 'retrieve' all of the visual information about the 3D world from the very limited information contained in the 2D retinal image? This is a basic and central question of perception, and many of the examples in this book will elucidate this process. Most illusions are artificially contrived, whether they come from a vision science laboratory or from the creative mind of an artist. They present stimuli that are greatly impoverished, lacking the wealth of contextual cues that would resolve their ambiguity. It is by exploring vision at these extreme limits that we slowly discover the various constraints that allow us to see a non-ambiguous scene.

Of course, there are also many other issues of perception, such as how do we perceive colour? How do we perceive motion? How do we attribute meaning to an image? How do we recognize faces? These are all very fundamental problems of perception.

Over the past fifty years, and especially during the last twenty years, there have been several different scientific groups rigorously studying and researching the problem of vision and perception from several different approaches. Some of these approaches have been conflicting, others have been supportive, others have been at cross-purposes, and some have been downright exclusionary. This is because, historically, researchers in visual physiology and visual psychophysics have disagreed on the appropriateness of their approaches. Often, those involved in the research find their own methodology to be so 'obviously' the correct one that they do not even bother to defend their choice of method. In this regard, some of the most significant and far-reaching controversies in the cognitive sciences have arisen not because there is a disagreement about the actual data, but about the relevance of the results and the choice of methods that were used to acquire them.

While researchers may not agree on the most useful approach to vision research, different methodologies are needed because the visual system processes information at many levels of sophistication. The physiologists have been mainly concerned with low-level vision, which deals with the functions of single neurons or small networks in early stages of the visual pathway. Psychophysicists have been working away at the other extreme, high-level vision, which includes cognitive processes that incorporate knowledge about objects, materials, and scenes. In between, there is an ill-defined region of mid-level vision, which involves the processing of surfaces, contours, depth, and so on.

For some time there appeared to be a good match between the physiologists, who were studying low-level vision processes, and the psychophysicists, who were studying higher-level visual processing. However, recently a number of leading psychophysicists have shown that many of the underlying neuronal mechanisms for various low-level effects, such as simultaneous contrast and brightness perception, which were previously thought to be well understood, may stand in need of revision. For example, changing the context of a scene can influence the responses of visual neurons, just as it changes what the observer sees. This means that many of the underlying mechanisms that mediate vision may be even 'messier' than previously thought, with cross-feedback from more than one level of visual processing contributing to processing at another level. Studying the visual system only at one level will never result in a full understanding of visual perception.

Fortunately, there is now an ever-growing number of vision scientists who are interested in not only the neuronal correlates of visual perception, but also in the psychology of vision. Visual perception is largely an ambiguity-solving process.

The task of vision scientists, therefore, is to uncover the hidden and underlying constraints, which have been so cleverly obscured, rather than to attribute to the visual system a degree of simplicity that it simply does not possess.

Yet sometimes our perceptions are wrong. Often these errors are classified as illusions and dismissed by many as failures of the visual system, quirky exceptions to normal vision. Descriptions of them in these terms have come from several eminent modern scientists. Marvin Minsky, regarded as the father of artificial intelligence, has called them 'bugs', pioneer researcher of visions and illusions, Richard Gregory, has labelled them 'mistakes', and Nobel prizewinner Francis Crick, who has recently been working on the problems associated with visual awareness, has put them down as 'partial failures'.

In fact, illusions are none of these things. The processes that underlie and mediate 'normal' vision are the same processes that give rise to illusions; to understand illusions is to understand normal visual processing. Many vision scientists study illusions because illusions can sometimes reveal the hidden constraints and complexities of the perceptual system in a way that normal perceptual processes do not. Indeed, there are numerous examples of how the study of illusions has led to important insights about perception and the visual system as a whole. For example, illusions such as the Hermann grid and Mach bands led to one of the earliest neuronal theories: that of lateral inhibition between nerve cells. In the nineteenth century an examination of colour after-effects led Hering to propose an 'opponent' process theory of colour vision. In physics, my original area of research, the part that doesn't fit in, or go as you expected, is the most interesting area to study.

If illusions are not failures of the visual system, then, what are they? After all, a number of different perceptual experiences are categorized as 'illusions'; what makes them fundamentally different from those we perceive as normal?

The first difference is a noticeable split between your perception and conception. With an illusion, your perception is fooled but your conception is correct – you're seeing something wrong (your mis-perception), but you know it's wrong (your correct conception). Initially, your conception may be fooled too, but at that point you are unaware that you are encountering an illusion. Only when your conception is at odds with your perception are you aware that you have encountered an illusion.

Furthermore, in almost all pictorial illusions (where the meaning of the image is not ambiguous), your perceptions will continue to be fooled, even though your conception is fine, no matter how many times you view the illusion. It does not matter how old you are, how smart you are, how cultured you are, or how artistic you are, you will be fooled by these illusions over and over again. In fact, you cannot 'undo' your incorrect perceptions, even with extensive experience, worldly knowledge or training. This will become quite evident as you go through the various examples in this book, and is a strong indication that your visual/perceptual system is highly constrained on how it interprets the world.

A related concept is the feeling of 'surprise' when you discover that your perception has been fooled, because your expectations were violated. Your sense of surprise, however, does not last with successive viewings of the same illusion. Many people also experience a certain joy in having their perceptions fooled. Of course, there are people who are also irritated, but the majority of people appear to have a pleasant experience when their expectations are misled; when, for example, they view a movie that has a clever plot twist or joke. Pleasure is the brain's way of rewarding us. Why we are 'rewarded' is an interesting question to ponder.

It is not my intention that the illusions included in this book should cause the reader to think that visual perception is unreliable and untrustworthy. This would be a mistake as, for the most part, our perceptions of the world are veridical – by and large, what you see is an accurate representation of the external world. However, our perception of the world is not a mirror image of reality, but an active, intelligent construct that allows us the best chances of survival in a complicated environment.

How we build our representation of reality is an incredibly complicated process. We do not have a clear or even generalized understanding of how we perceive our three-dimensional world, this in spite of over one hundred years of active research in vision and cognitive science.

This does not mean that we do not know anything. We have a tremendous wealth of accurate information about the structure and behaviour of the eye and the relevant parts of the brain, as well as of the biology of nerve cells and their many component molecules. What is not clearly understood is the process that mediates vision and perception. It is incredibly difficult to fit what we already know into a successful framework that explains how we have reached an explicit and fairly accurate mental representation of our world. Sometimes we get glimpses of this process; this book, if successful, will provide the reader with a few such glimpses. Scientists have achieved a great deal, but much more remains unknown.

Although this is a book about how we perceive illusions, in a much broader sense it is an introduction into thinking about how we see and perceive, and the hidden processes that underlie visual perception. All the effects presented here can be perceived without any scientific knowledge – they will work for all people with normal vision, generally above the age of five. As well as being an exciting area of current scientific research, the study of illusions can be immensely enjoyable. I hope that the examples and discussions offered here will stimulate you to think about the numerous questions that remain unanswered, including those concerning the greatest mystery of all – the human brain.

The perception of luminance or brightness would at first glance seem to be a straightforward task. All that is needed is to pass a photometer over a surface and measure the energy at each point; the more light coming from a particular part of the surface, the greater the measured value. Many photoreceptors in the retina respond in a similar way – the more light they receive, the more they are excited, and the greater is the firing rate in the ganglion cells to which they are connected. Yet, as we discover time and again, perception is much more complex than a simple one-to-one mapping of the external world from the retinal input. In the case of perceived brightness, our perception is definitely not a 'pixel-by-pixel' representation of differing light levels on the retina. Our perception of brightness can vary subjectively depending upon a variety of factors, including the context of the scene we are witnessing.

A white surface in dim light will give the same measured brightness value as a black surface in bright light. However, if enough of the context of the scene is visible, humans can usually distinguish between the two. In fact, the perceived lightness of real objects in a natural environment is largely independent of a whole range of illumination.

Furthermore, the perceived luminance or brightness of objects does not correspond in any simple way to their physical brightness. Two surfaces returning the same amount of light to the eye can look remarkably different. As will be demonstrated in this chapter, there are no physical differences in luminance. There is, however, a difference between the stimulus and your perception of that stimulus.

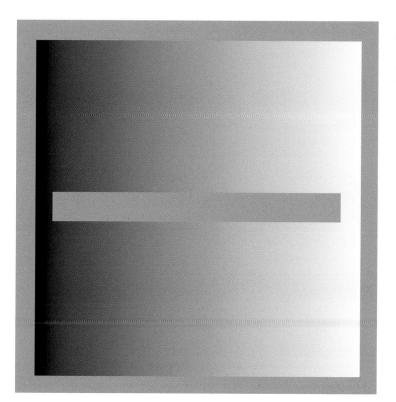

A Simultaneous Contrast Illusion

Is the horizontal bar the same value of grey throughout?

An Assimilation Illusion

Does the grey centre square appear darker than its grey surround?

White's Illusion

Do the grey vertical bars appear identical or different?

The Chevreul Illusion

In the Chevreul illusion, each step from light to dark has a uniform brightness within the step. But at a border going from light to dark, the light edge makes the dark edge next to it appear even darker. Put a pencil over the edge between any two stripes and the adjoining stripes will appear the same.

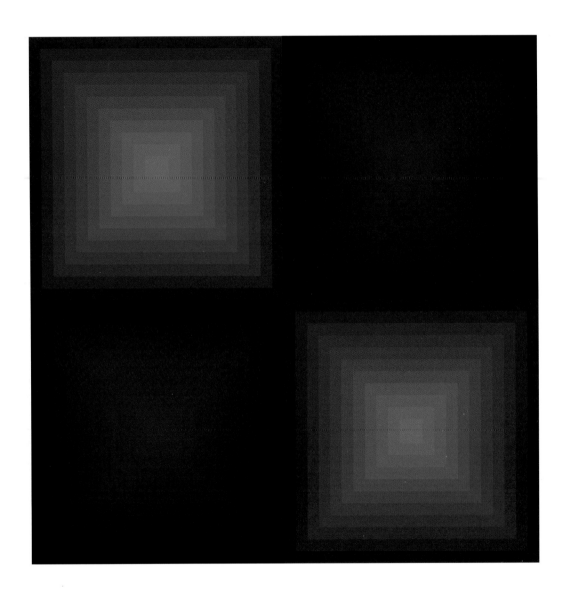

Vasarely's Illusion

Do you perceive a bright diagonal 'cross' within each of the coloured squares?

The Diamond Variation of the Craik-O'Brien-Cornsweet Illusion

Look at each row of diamonds. Does each row appear darker than the row above it?

Purves and Lotto's Contrast Illusion

Look at the striped figure. It appears to be made of two grey stripes that lie in between three white stripes. Yet, what you see is not what you got! The two grey stripes on the top of the figure are identical in luminance to the three white stripes on the front of the figure.

Adelson's Checkerboard and Shadow Illusion

Examine the checkerboard pattern of both light and dark checks. Do the 'light' checks inside the shadow appear the same shade of grey as the 'dark' checks outside the shadow?

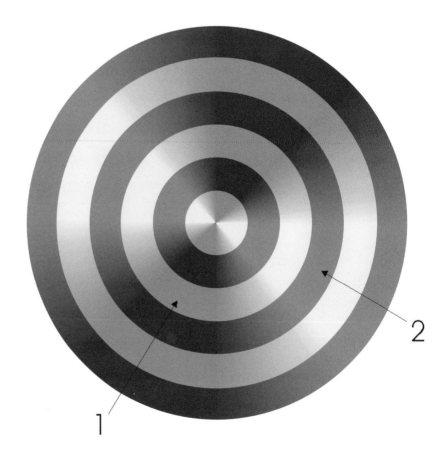

Todorovic's Dartboard Illusion

Do the 'light' and 'dark' regions, as indicated by the arrows, appear to be different? Believe it or not, they are identical.

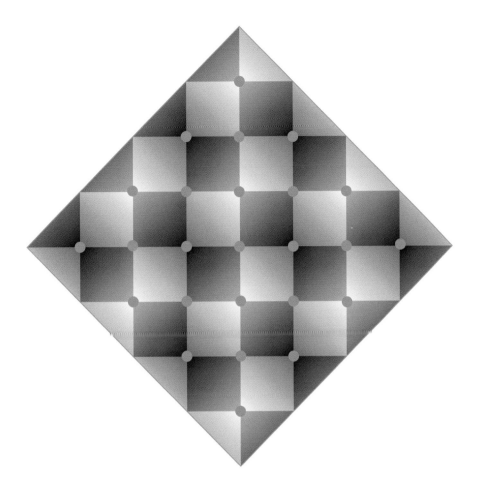

Todorovic's Gradient Chessboard Illusion

The gradients are real, but the small disks all have the same luminance, even though some appear light, middle, and dark grey.

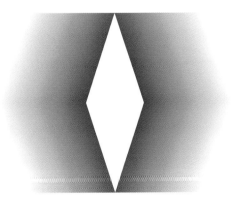
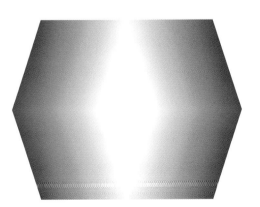

Bressen's Double Brilliant Illusion

Does one diamond appear whiter than the other?

The Ehrenstein Figure

Do you perceive circles, even though there is no edge to define them? Do these circles appear brighter?

BRIGHTNESS and CONTRAST ILLUSIONS
What's going on?

A Simultaneous Contrast Illusion

Yes, the horizontal bar is identical throughout. You can check this by covering everything except the horizontal bar. This indicates that the surrounding values of grey influence your perception of the grey value of the bar – a dark grey surround means the appearance of a lighter bar. This is known as a simultaneous contrast illusion.

An Assimilation Illusion

The grey value of both the centre square and its surround are identical. This is an example of assimilation, the opposite of simultaneous contrast. The grey of the centre square (between the black lines) looks darker than the grey that surrounds it (between the white lines). In fact, the same grey was used over the whole surface of the picture. This consistency can be confirmed by hiding the ends of the white or black lines near one of the corners of the small square.

White's Illusion

The grey vertical bars are identical in value. The grey segments that replace the black parts of the black bars look much brighter than the grey segments that replace parts of the white bars. This is surprising: because of local simultaneous contrast, the grey patches that are surrounded by white should appear darker than the ones surrounded by black.

White's illusion only occurs when the luminance of the grey patches lies between the range of minimum and maximum values of the inducing stripes (long white and black stripes).

The Chevreul Illusion

Each stripe from light to dark has a uniform brightness within the stripe, but increases from one stripe to another in staircase fashion. At a border going from light to dark, the light edge makes the dark edge next to it appear even darker, and the stripes appear scalloped.

The illusion is named after Michel Chevreul (1786-1889), a well-known French chemist, who was later to become extremely influential in the world of art, specifically Pointillism and Divisionism. He was hired as director of the dye plant of Gobelin Tapestry Works in Paris, where he had to respond to many complaints about the substandard quality of dyes. Many complaints were legitimate, but others he found were due to an illusion of colour contrast. He discovered that the appearance of a yarn was determined not only by the colour with which it was dyed, but by the colours of the surrounding yarns. Chevreul investigated the specifics of this

phenomenon and established the rules that describe the influence of the surrounding context on the perceived colour of a target. He first described this illusion in 1839.

Vasarely's Illusion

The brighter diagonal areas are of the same luminance as the diamonds on which they rest. In other words, if you were to measure any of the concentric strips with a photometer, you would find that the same amount of light is reflected from all points along any one strip, which of course, includes the part of the strip along the diagonal that appears brighter. This illusion may result from the lateral inhibition in the retina and other early stages of visual processing.

This illusion was created by Hungarian/French 'Op' artist Victor Vasarely, who was quite fond of putting simultaneous contrast effects into his artworks.

The Diamond Variation of the Craik-O'Brien-Cornsweet Illusion

All the diamond shapes in this figure are identical in luminance, but when combined in a tessellated pattern the diamonds near the bottom are perceived as darker than those near the top of the figure. There is a rapid change from the light to the dark on both sides of a border that is propagated and creates grey levels, the averages of which differ on the two sides of the border.

Vision scientists Isao Watanabe, Patrick Cavanagh, and Stuart Anstis described this very effective Craik-O'Brien-Cornsweet variation with diamond shapes for the first time in 1995.

Purves and Lotto's Contrast Illusion

In this dramatic brightness illusion, Dale Purves and R. Beau Lotto show that there is a dramatic increase in the saliency of the simultaneous contrast effect when mutually consistent information that indicates that some of the stripes are in deep shadow and others are in intense light is put into the scene.

Adelson's Checkerboard and Shadow Illusion

The light check within the shadow is identical to the dark check outside the shadow. You can test this by covering everything except those two squares or looking at them through a peephole. MIT vision scientist Ted Adelson created this remarkable brightness illusion to show that scene interpretation has an effect on perceived

brightness. According to Adelson, the visual system needs to determine the colour of objects in the world. In this case the problem is to determine the grey shade of the checks on the floor. Just measuring the luminance is not enough: a cast shadow will dim a surface, so that a white surface in shadow may be reflecting less light than a black surface in full light. The visual system uses several constraints to determine where the shadows are and how to compensate for them, in order to determine the shade of grey 'paint' that belongs to the surface.

The first constraint is based on local contrast. In shadow or not, a check that is lighter than its neighbouring checks is probably lighter than average, and vice versa. In the figure, the light check in shadow is surrounded by darker checks. Thus, even though the check is physically dark, it is light when compared to its neighbours. The dark checks outside the shadow, conversely, are surrounded by lighter checks, so they look dark by comparison.

A second constraint is based on the fact that shadows often have soft or fuzzy edges, while paint boundaries (like the checks) often have sharp edges. The visual system tends to ignore gradual changes in light level, so that it can determine the colour of the surfaces without being misled by shadows. In this case, the shadow has a fuzzy edge, and the cylinder appears to be casting a shadow consistent with experience.

Todorovic's Gradient Chessboard Illusion

This is a new brightness illusion created by Hungarian vision scientist Dejan Todorovic.

Bressen's Double Brilliant Illusion

The two diamonds are identical in luminance. If the diamonds have the same luminance, but the one on the left has a larger luminance ratio with its surround, and the surrounds are both locally white, the target on the right will appear to be lighter. Italian vision scientist Paula Bressen discovered this illusion in 2000.

The Ehrenstein Figure

A set of radial lines whose ends form a subjective circle will induce a positive brightness contrast, with the subjective circle being perceived as being brighter than the ground.

Walter Ehrenstein discovered the illusion in 1941.

Images that appear to scintillate or twinkle when you make eye movements across them are a subclass of simultaneous contrast illusions, which you came across in the previous chapter.

In its most basic form, this type of illusion was first noticed by Reverend W. Selwyn and reported by the British physicist Sir David Brewster in 1844. However, in 1870 the German physiologist Ludimar Hermann was the first to attribute the effect to simultaneous contrast between the image and its background, and so the illusion was named after him. A variation of the Hermann Grid Illusion was first demonstrated at a vision conference in 1993, by J.R. Bergen. The following year a still more powerful version was discovered, by Elke Lingelbach, and called the Scintillating Grid Illusion.

Many 'Op' artists in the 1970s, such as Victor Vasarely, Bridget Riley and Nicholas Wade, incorporated these types of simultaneous contrast effects into their artworks.

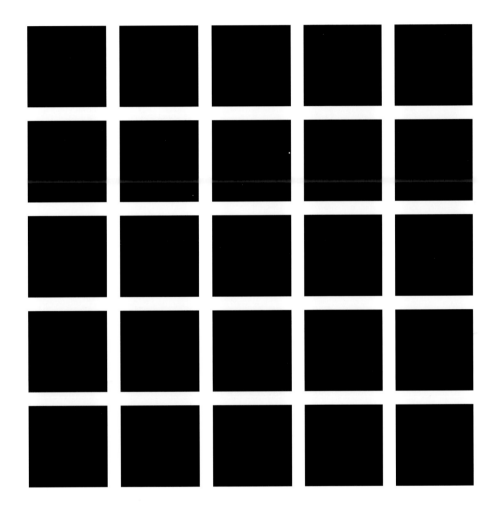

The Hermann Grid Illusion

Do you see ghostly grey dots at the intersections? Stare at any one of them and it will disappear. What happens to the strength of the illusion when you tilt the image by 45°? Try looking at the figure from differing distances. What happens to the strength of the illusion?

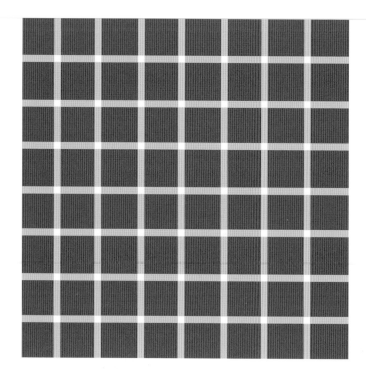

A Modified Hermann Grid

Move your eyes about this image. Around the spot on which the eye is fixed, the intersections remain white. Away from this point they flash lilac; as the eye scans the picture, the coloured areas move, too. When the distance from which the picture is viewed is increased, their number multiplies.

The Coloured Scintillating Grid Illusion

Move your eyes about this image, and the junctions will appear to scintillate and change their distribution.

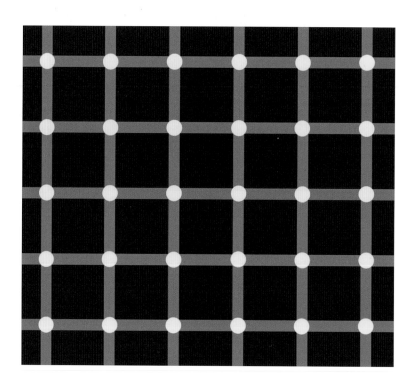

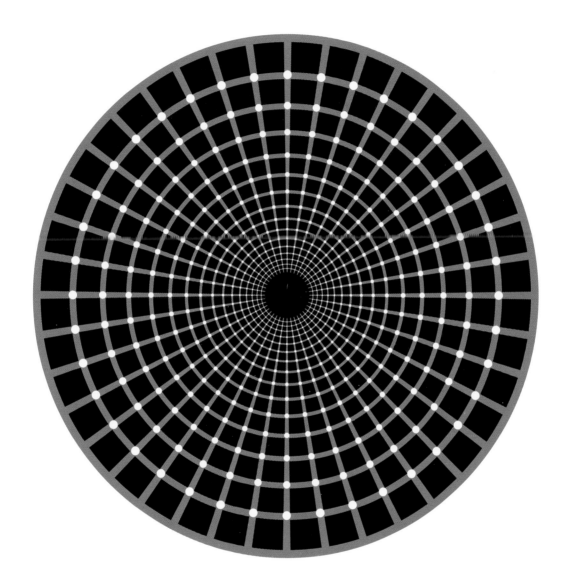

A Quirky Variation of the Scintillating Grid Illusion

In this variation of the scintillating grid illusion, illusory black dots abruptly appear or disappear in white circles when you move your eyes around the image. However, if you fixate at the centre, the white circles will disappear.

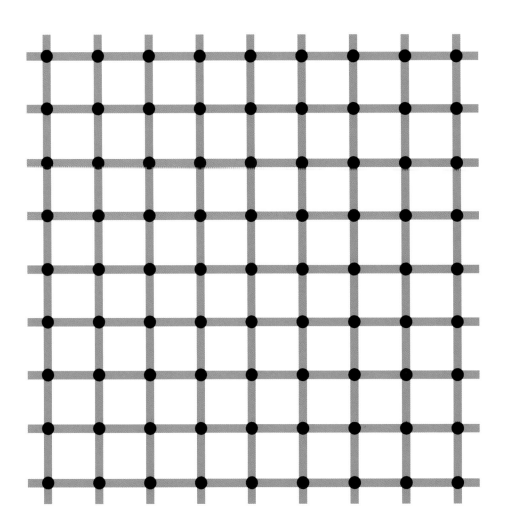

The Scintillating Grid Illusion

Move your eyes around this image, and the junctions will appear to scintillate and change their distribution. Like the standard Hermann grid illusion, if you stare at any intersection, the flashing will cease in that area. This illusion works best with peripheral vision viewed at arm's length.

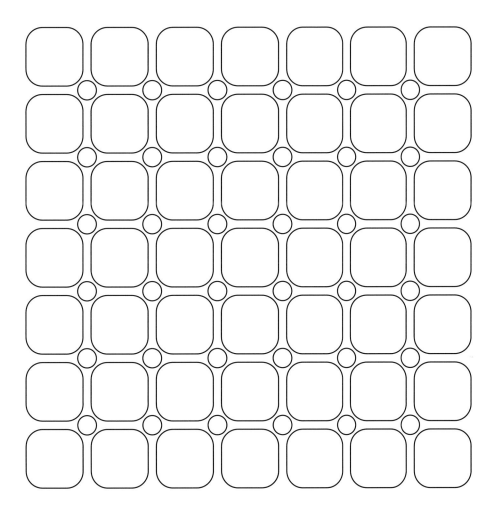

Compression of the Scintillating Grid Illusion

If you scan this image, a small black dot appears in each circle. Japanese vision scientist and artist Akiyoshi Kitaoka created this variation on the scintillating grid illusion in 2002.

Pinna's Scintillating Lustre Illusion

Do these circles appear to scintillate?

Kitaoka's Gunjo Scintillating Illusion

The blue dots are identical between the left and right figures. The dots of the left figure appear to scintillate reddish blue while the dots of the right figure appear to twinkle greenish blue.

Morellet's Tiret Illusion

Move your eyes around this image and small circles will appear to scintillate and fade.

What's going on?

The Hermann Grid Illusion

There are several features of the Hermann grid: (1) Spots appear at intersections. (2) Spots disappear when you stare directly at them, depending on the viewing distance. (3) The strength of the illusion depends on the dimensions of the bars. (4) The illusion grows in strength with the number of intersections. (5) The illusion is weakened if the image is tilted at 45°.

The generally accepted explanation for this effect is based on the assumption that the width of the lines on the Hermann grid produces an image on the retina that is just equal to the diameter of the centre of a simple circular receptive field found in a retinal ganglion cell. In this way, the lateral inhibition network can account for most aspects of this illusion. Therefore, the Hermann grid is classified as a simultaneous contrast illusion.

Eye movements are not required to elicit the illusion, but with fixation and subsequent adaptation, the illusion quickly diminishes.

A Modified Hermann Grid

In this modification of the classic Hermann grid illusion, the intersection points are coloured white rather than yellow. This leads to the occurrence of a new colour effect, indicating colour contrast mechanisms.

The Coloured Scintillating Grid Illusion

Experiments have shown that the scintillating grid illusion works with the following configurations: (a) grids with coloured backgrounds and grey lines, (b) grids with a black background and coloured lines, and (c) grids with complementary colours and backgrounds. Every grid induced scintillating coloured illusory spots.

A Quirky Variation of the Scintillating Grid Illusion

This is a quirky variation of the scintillating grid illusion discovered in 2002 by American vision scientists Michael Levine and J. Jason McAnany. This is a complex perceptual effect that occurs only under specific circumstances. It may be related to other forms of 'visual disappearance' and is termed 'blanking'. It is not fully understood what causes the disappearance, which is no doubt due to a different underlying mechanism than the scintillation effect. Japanese vision researcher and artist Akiyoshi Kitaoka created this version of the illusion.

The Scintillating Grid Illusion

The scintillating grid illusion is identical to the Hermann grid illusion, except that the black squares are separated by grey (instead of white) lines, and there is a white circle filling each intersection to cancel the illusory spots of the Hermann grid. These seemingly subtle differences dramatically change the illusion in a number of ways, and make its effect more powerful.

In the case of the scintillating grid illusion, there are probably some small timing differences between centre and surround responses. The centre responses are quicker and more transient than the surround responses, which cause the dots at the intersections to scintillate. As we scan the image, the cells that signal white at the intersections first give a strong centre signal in response to the white dots at the intersections, but then their signal is weakened, as the surround inhibition takes place. This reduction is perceived as a darkening of the spot.

Elke Lingelbach discovered the scintillating grid illusion in 1994 (although a weaker version was first demonstrated at a vision conference in 1993 by J.R. Bergen).

Pinna's Scintillating Lustre Illusion

This is a brand new illusion, which is called the scintillating lustre illusion. It is a modification of the Ehrenstein brightness illusion (see the example in the brightness chapter) and the standard scintillating grid. It appears to arise from a competition between the ON (brightness) and OFF (darkness) visual subsystems. Italian vision scientist Baingio Pinna and German vision scientist Lothar Spillman discovered it in 2002.

Kitaoka's Gunjo Scintillating Illusion

This version of the scintillating grid illusion incorporates colour assimilation mechanisms. Japanese vision scientist and artist Akiyoshi Kitaoka created this variation on the scintillating grid illusion in 2002.

Morellet's Tiret Illusion

Your visual system tends to prefer organization and groups, so it searches for the 'best' interpretation. In most images there is a way to group and organize the image. However, in 'Tirets' by French artist François Morellet, there is no 'best' interpretation. Rather, there are lots of possible circles. As you scan this image, your visual system is constantly searching for the 'best' interpretation; however, many continuously arise.

*T*hese are some of the most powerful illusions known. There are several well-known varieties, each having its own striking effect. Twisted cord illusions were first discovered in the late nineteenth century by mat weavers, who noticed a distortion in their patterns. In 1894, the pioneering German psychologist Hugo Münsterberg was called in to investigate the phenomenon, which he called the 'shifted checkerboard figure'.

In 1908, James Fraser, a British psychologist, published a paper entitled 'A New Visual Illusion of Direction'. In it he showed how one could adapt the figures discovered by Münsterberg into a powerful new illusion of direction – the twisted cord. Fraser called the basic unit of his figures, a line with a triangle at either end, a 'directional unit'. He maintained that this directional unit was very effective at misleading the direction of the visual system. Fraser used this unit on both straight and curved figures, the latter being the famous Fraser Spiral Illusion. Since Fraser's initial discovery there have been endless variations of illusory spiral patterns created out of concentric circles. A related twisted cord illusion was later discovered on the wall of a nineteenth-century café located in Bristol (Café Wall illusion).

Twisted cord illusions have been the subject of considerable theoretical interest and empirical investigation. Recently, the Japanese vision scientist and 'Op' artist Akiyoshi Kitaoka has created a whole new range of powerful twisted cord illusions based on his investigation of this effect.

The Twisted Cord Illusion
Do the vertical lines appear to bend?

The Café Wall Illusion

This is the wall of an English café in Bristol, where the café wall illusion was first discovered. Do you perceive the illusionary wedges?

The Fraser Spiral Illusion

Do you perceive a spiral or a series of concentric circles?

Wilcox's Twisted Circle Illusion

Do you perceive a series of warped circles?

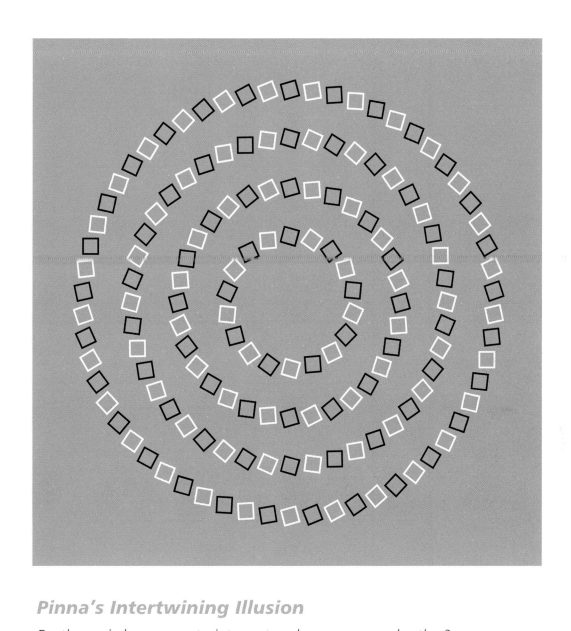

Pinna's Intertwining Illusion

Do these circles appear to intersect and cross over each other?

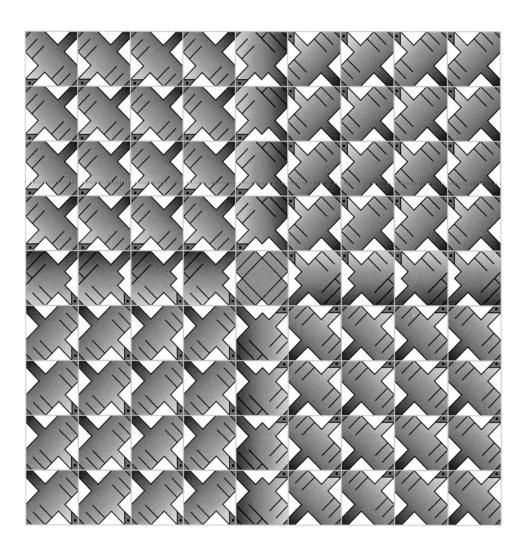

Kitaoka's Café Escher Illusion

Do the squares appear to bulge in the centre? Check them with a straight edge.

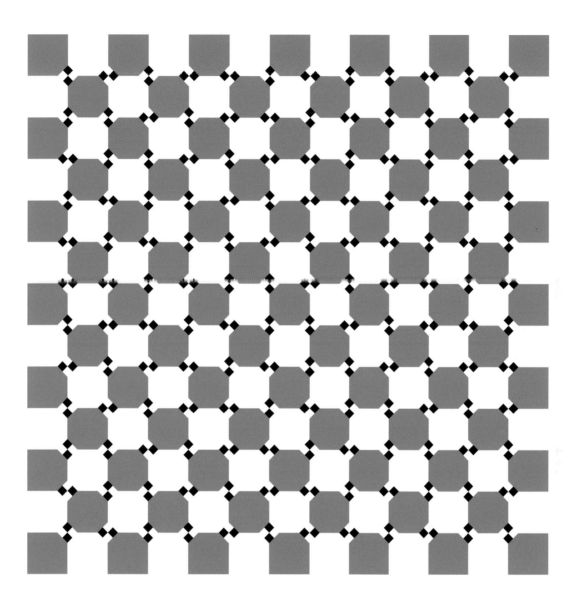

Kitaoka's Distorted Figure

The vertical or horizontal edges appear to be distorted and the figure to be wavy.

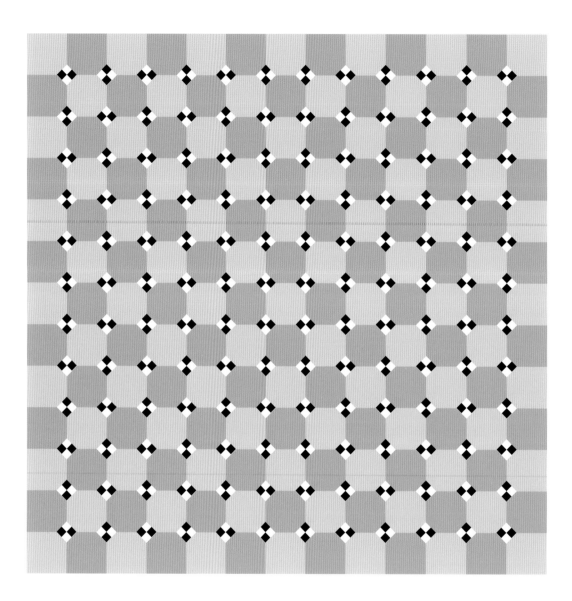

Men with Sunglasses

Vertical or horizontal edges appear to be distorted and each quarter region appears to move.

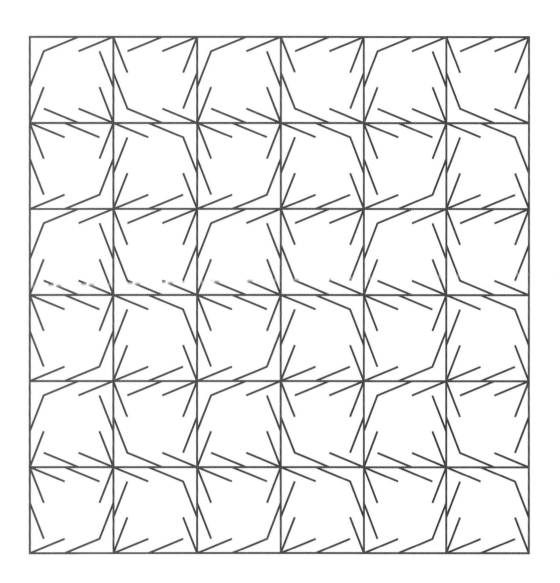

The Zöllner Illusion

The horizontal lines are parallel, but appear to tilt.

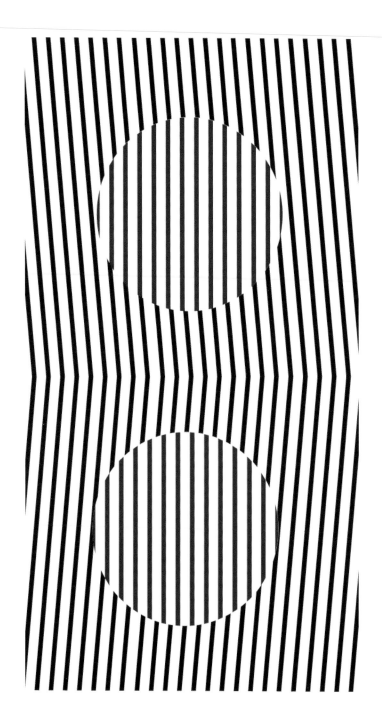

Blackmore's Tilt Orientation Illusion

Do the vertical red lines in the two centre sections appear tilted with respect to their surrounds?

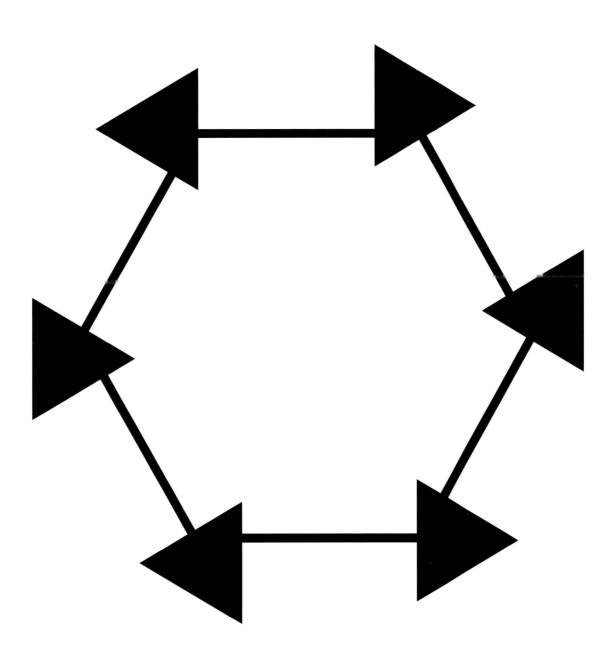

Gerbino's Illusion

*Do the straight-line segments, if connected, appear
to form a perfect hexagon?*

TWISTED CORD ILLUSIONS
What's going on?

The Twisted Cord Illusion
The lines are perfectly vertical and parallel to each other. The illusion is likely due to orientation-sensitive simple cells in the striate cortex, which interact to combine closely-spaced tilted lines into a single tilted line.

The Café Wall Illusion
The horizontal lines are parallel and the wedges are illusory. Prominent vision researchers Richard L. Gregory and Priscilla Heard first reported the Café Wall illusion in 1979. A member of Gregory's lab had noticed that the front of a café (St Michael's Hill, Bristol, England) had been adorned with black and white ceramic tiles. The mortar between adjacent rows of tiles was visually apparent, and the black/white pattern was offset by half a tile width in alternating rows.

The Fraser Spiral Illusion
This is not a spiral, but actually a series of concentric circles. The spiral is made out of a series of overlapping arc segments within several concentric circles of diminishing size. The Fraser spiral illusion is so strong that it can even induce incorrect finger tracing! Knowledge of its true nature or successive experience with it will not dramatically decrease its effect.

The strength of the illusion, however, will be greatly diminished if you cover up half of the illustration. This means that the illusion is due to global image processing and grouping of the scene's context. In this particular case, the perceived 'twist' at each portion of the circle is transmitted across the entire circle to produce the spiral effect. Therefore, spirals are perceived whenever lines producing tilt illusions in a coherent direction are converted into concentric circles.

The Fraser spiral is related to other twisted cord illusions, and is among the most complex in this category of illusions. Some additional factors are involved in the visual processing of this illusion. James Fraser, a British psychologist, first discovered it in 1906.

Wilcox's Twisted Circle Illusion
This is a variation of the Fraser spiral, and also consists of concentric circles. James Wilcox, a twelve-year-old artist, created it.

Pinna's Intertwining Illusion
This is a new type of directional illusion discovered recently by Italian vision scientist Baingio Pinna. It is not yet understood what causes this effect, although the orientation polarity of the elements, the observation distance, and the geometrical distance between the elements is very important. If you change the polarity between the two rings made up of squares, the intertwined effect will be perceived as a spiral.

Kitaoka's Café Escher Illusion
This is an entirely new variation of the twisted cord illusion by Japanese vision scientist and 'Op' artist Akiyoshi Kitaoka entitled 'The Café Escher Illusion'.

Kitaoka's Distorted Figure
This is another new twisted cord variation by Akiyoshi Kitaoka.

Men with Sunglasses
This twisted cord illusion by Akiyoshi Kitaoka also exhibits a relative motion.

The Zöllner Illusion
In the last century, there were a number of distortion illusions produced by the intersection of hatched lines. Johann Zöllner, who discovered this illusion in 1860, sparked an international interest in the study of optical illusions, and scores of papers have been published about it.

Zöllner thought that the illusion is strongest when the hatching lines are inclined at 45° to the main lines. Yet, further studies have shown that the illusion is at its maximum when the intersecting angle is 10 to 30°. Some references claimed that any angle from 0 to 90° gives this illusion, but this was not supported by other references. Japanese vision scientists Kitaoka and Ishihara have recently provided evidence that the Zöllner illusion is formed by three elemental illusions: two are acute-angle expansion illusions and the other is an acute-angle contraction illusion. One of the expansion illusions is of a local type while the rest are of global types.

Blackmore's Tilt Orientation Illusion
The lines are both vertical and parallel.

It is not clear what causes this illusion, which is related to the Zöllner illusion, but one theory is based on the fact that there are inhibitory interactions among orientation selective neurons in the primary visual cortex (V1). In other words, some cells respond more strongly to differences than to similarities in a visual scene. This can exaggerate the lines' orientations. Neural inhibition is a powerful tool for building up features of scenes, but here inhibition is given a rather different role. This illusion was first described by English vision scientist Colin Blackmore in 1973 and is also related to the Tilt After-effect.

Gerbino's Illusion
The lines, if connected, would form a perfect hexagon. The points where they would connect are 'masked' by the triangles. The visual system tends to continue lines when they disappear behind an occluding object, as they do in this case. The end point of each segment appears to be near the centre of each triangle, which causes the perception of misalignment. Italian vision scientist Walter Gerbino discovered this illusion.

4 FIGURE and GROUND ILLUSIONS

It is highly important that your visual system can interpret the patterns on your retina in terms of external objects. To do this it needs to be able to distinguish objects (figure) from their background (ground). This is such an important perceptual process that your visual system has developed quite a number of rules to distinguish a figure from its background. Most of the time it is relatively easy, and difficulties only arise when an attempt is made to conceal an object through the use of natural or artificial camouflage.

In this chapter, we examine some figure/ground illusions where the distinction between an object and its figure has been deliberately obscured or made ambiguous. In many of these illusions, by manipulating various contours and rules that the visual system has developed to disambiguate figure from ground, one can create images where the figure can be interchanged with the ground. In these cases, both the figure and the ground will have meaningful interpretations, which causes a perceptual 'flip-flop'.

Figure/ground illusions have been popular since the late nineteenth century, and appeared on various puzzle cards, postcards, and in advertisements through the twentieth century. Interestingly, many of these images influenced the original Gestalt psychologists to study various aspects of perception and grouping.

Hidden Profile of a Queen and her Husband

Can you find the profiles of Queen Elizabeth II and her husband Prince Phillip?

The Original Face/Vase Illusion

It should be easy to see the goblet, but can you find the two profiles?

Can You Find Both the Figure and the Ground?

The words 'Figure' and 'Ground' are both written here. Can you find them?

Tools

Can you find the missing tools?

A Sudden Change of Direction

Stare at the fish in this illustration and they will face left and then suddenly change direction and face right.

Sara Nader

Can you find the face of the woman that the man is serenading? This figure/ground illusion is by Roger Shepard.

A Mouse Playing Hide and Seek with a Cat

Is the cat hiding from the mouse or the mouse hiding from the cat? This reversible photo illusion was created by digital artist Alice Klarke, based on an original drawing by English artist Peter Brooks.

Saint George and the Dragon

Can you find both a portrait of Saint George and a depiction of his slaying of the dragon?

The Ghost of Napoleon Standing by His Tomb

Can you find the standing figure of Napoleon?

Corporal Violet

Can you find the three profiles (Napoleon, his wife and son) hidden between the leaves? This card, whose artist is unknown, originated around 1815.

Vanity

Can you see the skull?

Beckoning Balustrade

Can you find the figures hiding in between the columns? This figure/ground illusion is by Roger Shepard.

What's going on?

The Original Face/Vase Illusion

You can see the two profiles on either side of the vase if you turn the card upside down. This American puzzle card was published in 1880. The pedigree of this illusion, however, is even older. Examples can be found in eighteenth century French prints, in which the portraits not only define a vase, usually in a naturalistic setting, but the profiles themselves differ, each representing a particular person.

Can You Find Both the Figure and the Ground?

The darker 'ground' spells 'Ground'. Stanford psychologist Roger Shepard created this figure/ground illusion.

Saint George and the Dragon

This figure/ground illusion is by Sandro Del Prete. Look at Saint George's hair to see the battle scene.

The Ghost of Napoleon Standing by His Tomb

Napoleon is hiding in between the trees. Shortly after Napoleon died, there were many such versions of this illusion depicting his ghost standing over his grave.

Vanity

Charles Gilbert, an American magazine illustrator some time around 1905, created this classic illusion, entitled 'All is Vanity'. It was a very popular motif that was imitated many times, including by the Spanish surrealist Salvador Dalí.

The oldest known category of illusions consists of simple geometrical figures that involve an estimation of either extent or area. Most of these figures were discovered in the mid to late nineteenth century. Scores of scientific studies have been devoted to them. To date, no theory has been able to fully explain these simple illusions, despite the fact that the illusions are constant for almost all observers.

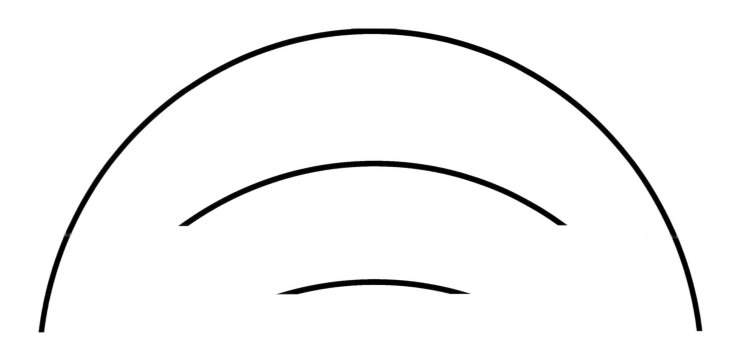

Tolansky's Curvature Illusion

Are the three arc segments identical in curvature?

The Wundt Illusion

Which old lady appears larger?

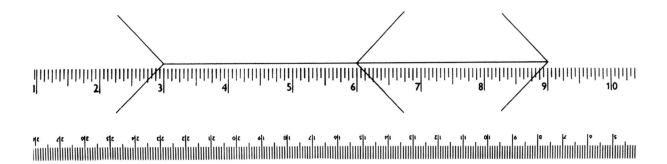

The Müller-Lyer Illusion

Which line segment appears longer?

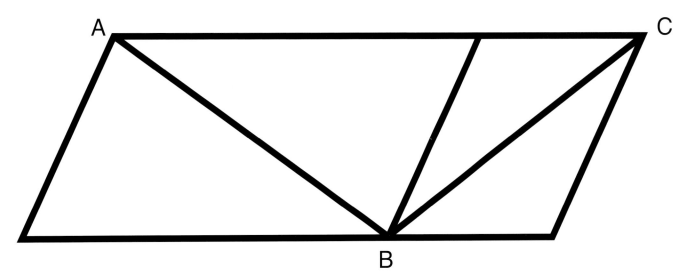

Sander's Parallelogram

Does the line AB appear longer than BC?

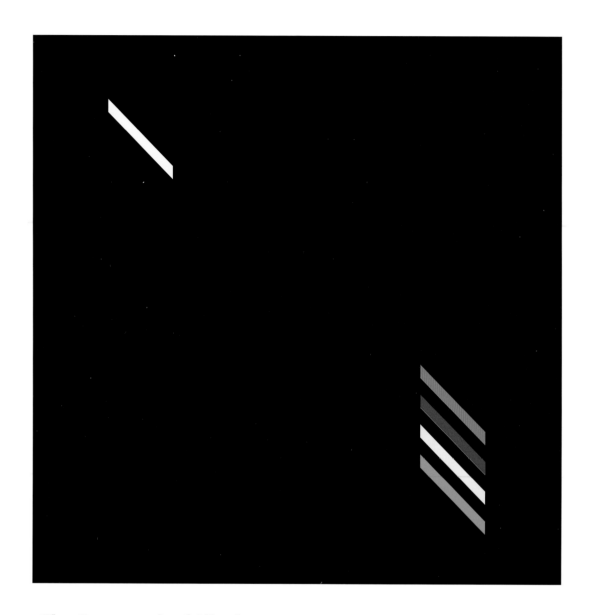

The Poggendorf Illusion

Which coloured line intersects with the white line?

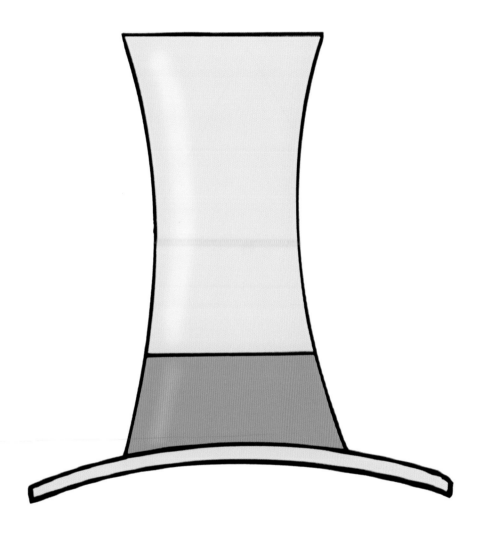

The Top Hat Illusion

Does the height of the hat appear longer than its width?

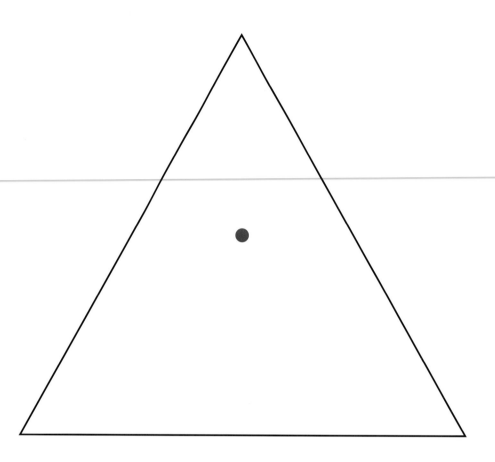

A Height Estimation Illusion

Does the red dot appear more than halfway up the height of the triangle?

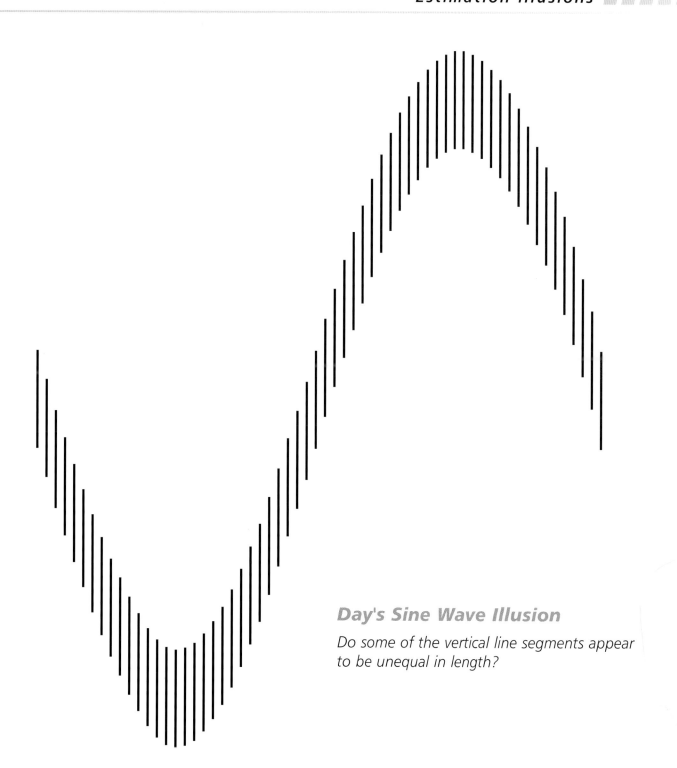

Day's Sine Wave Illusion

Do some of the vertical line segments appear to be unequal in length?

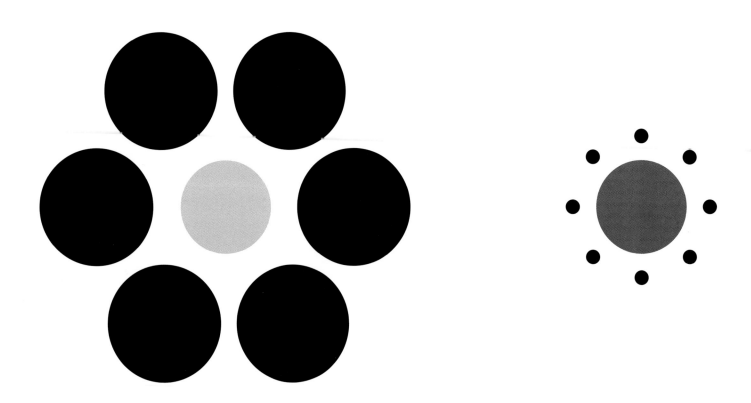

The Ebbinghaus Illusion

Which inner circle appears larger in size?

Tolansky's Curvature Illusion

The three arc segments appear to have widely differing curvatures, but they are all identical in curvature. The bottom two segments are just shorter arc segments of the top segment. The earliest visual receptors only interpret the world in terms of short line segments. Curvature is perceived when the relative positions of these line segments are summed across a large area of space. So, when given a small segment of a curve, your visual system cannot accurately detect its curvature.

Another rival theory to account for this illusion, involves assimilation. According to the assimilation theory, when two objects in a visual array are compared in size, an individual will perceive each object as the average size of the other objects involved. The assimilation theory states that since the longer arc of the second segment is placed next to the shorter arc of the first, the entire second arc will appear longer.

The Wundt Illusion

The two figures are absolutely identical in size and shape. This illusion, discovered by Wilhelm Wundt in the nineteenth century, is similar to the curvature illusion described in the previous example.

The Müller-Lyer Illusion

Both segments are equal in length. When the fins are inward, it causes an underestimation of size, and when they are outward, it causes an overestimation of size. This classic is probably the most famous and reprinted of all illusions, since its first introduction in 1889. Since that time there has been an enormous proliferation of theories to explain it; however, there is still no satisfactory explanation to date to account for the effect.

Sander's Parallelogram

The line segments are equal. This illusion produces a greater illusion of extent than the classic Müller-Lyer illusion, although it is not understood why. The illusion was discovered in 1926.

The Poggendorf Illusion

The white line intersects with the yellow line, even though you may not perceive it that way.

The Poggendorf illusion is one of the most famous distortion illusions known. While it is over 140 years old, there have been no end of theories to try to account for it. Recently, interactive versions have revealed new characteristics and variations of this illusion. There is, unfortunately, no theory to date that will adequately account for all the variations perceived. It is worthwhile, however, to examine the most popular theory advanced so far to explain this illusion.

A theory that was popular for many years, which had its origins in the theories of the nineteenth-century physicist Hermann von Helmholtz, and even had a neuronal underpinning, was based on the overestimation of acute angles. It was suggested that we have orientation detectors that exaggerate all acute angles and minimize all obtuse angles. This theory has its basis in the exciting work of Hubel and Wiesel who discovered that cells in the visual cortex of a cat 'detect' contour orientation on the retina.

Hubel and Wiesel, who recorded activity from single cells of the area striata of the cat's brain while presenting the cat with simple visual shapes, found that some cells were only active when a bar of light was presented at a certain angle. Different cells would respond to different angles. The presence of an adjacent contour of a different orientation would have the effect of lateral inhibition, where activity on one nerve cell reduced the effect on adjacent neurons.

While the overestimation of acute angles occurs in some distortion illusions, it does not fully explain what is going on in the Poggendorf illusion. This is particularly evident when we get rid of the middle bar. The illusion is still present, even though there is no actual vertical contour to form acute or obtuse angles. There is no contour present that can be attributed to lateral inhibition of the contour-orientation cells.

As another control, one can eliminate either the acute or obtuse angles and see how the illusion is affected. The illusion remains when one removes the acute angle; however, removing the obtuse angle has little or no effect.

The Poggendorf illusion was actually derived from another famous illusion – the Zöllner illusion. In 1860, J. C. Poggendorf, the editor of a journal of physics and chemistry, received a monograph from F. Zöllner, an astronomer, that described an illusion he accidentally noticed on a cloth pattern. Zöllner's illusion shows that parallel lines intersected by a pattern of short diagonal lines appear to diverge.

Poggendorf noticed and described another effect of the apparent misalignment of the diagonal lines in Zöllner's figure. Thus the Poggendorf illusion was discovered.

The Top Hat Illusion

The height of the hat and its width are the same. This is a variation of the classic inverted T illusion, which has been attributed to Johann Oppel. Oppel produced several original patterns of his own, and was largely responsible for creating an interest in the studying of simple optical illusions. Yet, the inverted T illusion originates from A. Fick, a physiologist who described it in his doctoral thesis in 1851. This is perhaps the first geometrical optical illusion created. It is not fully understood what causes this effect. However, the illusion persists if the figure is rotated 90°, so it is not due to asymmetry of the retina, as one witless psychologist asserted.

A Height Estimation Illusion

The red dot is located halfway up the triangle, although it appears to be much higher. This is a variation of the inverted T illusion, in which vertical lines are judged to be of greater extent than horizontal lines of the same length. The illusion also works in an L configuration.

Day's Sine Wave Illusion

All the lengths are equal.

The Ebbinghaus Illusion

The inner circles are identical in size, even though the circle with the smaller ones surrounding it appears bigger and the converse is also true. However, this effect decreases as the distance between the larger and smaller circles increases.

This illusion is caused by a misjudgement of area. Your visual system often assesses size through contrast with other objects in the visual field.

Although it is possible to determine our perception of colour objectively, by means of a device that measures its wavelength, this whole area is very complex and not well understood. A basic role of perception is to differentiate figures from their backgrounds. In the visual world, colour differences may provide additional means of distinguishing between foreground and background.

If you have tried to purchase a car at night, you will know that lighting conditions can have a profound effect on it. Similarly, artists know that surrounding colours can dramatically influence our perception of a single colour under consideration. Contextual cues can also alter our perception of colour. For example, when you see fairy lights reflected on a wall, the colours you perceive may not be the ones that are really there. The brain can compensate for the direction that the lights are coming from, which means you see a colour closer to that of the light bulb than the light that is being reflected directly off the wall. In effect, our visual system takes into account the physics of the light that strikes the object to determine the colour of the object. Colour is assigned to an object only after the visual system has taken into account how light is reflected off of it.

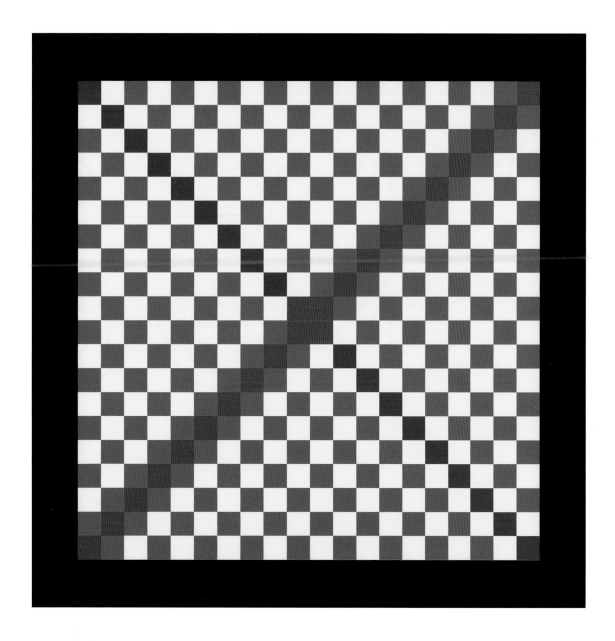

Colour Assimilation

Do both diagonal lines of red squares appear the same shade of red?

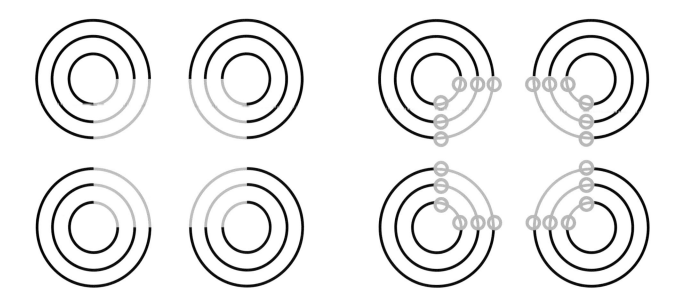

Neon Colour Spreading

Do you perceive a faint bluish colour within the square region on the left?

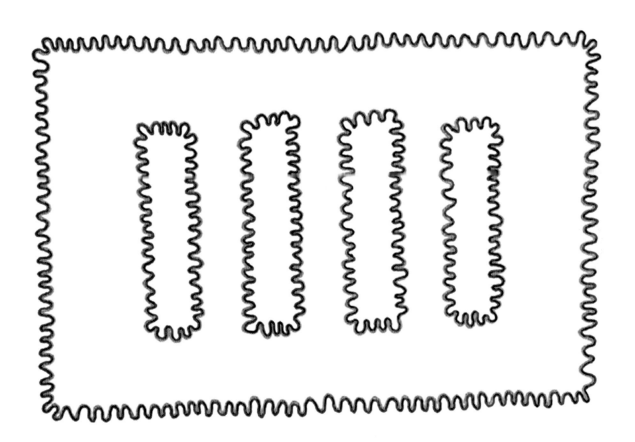

Pinna's Watercolour Effect

Do you perceive colour within the bordered area?

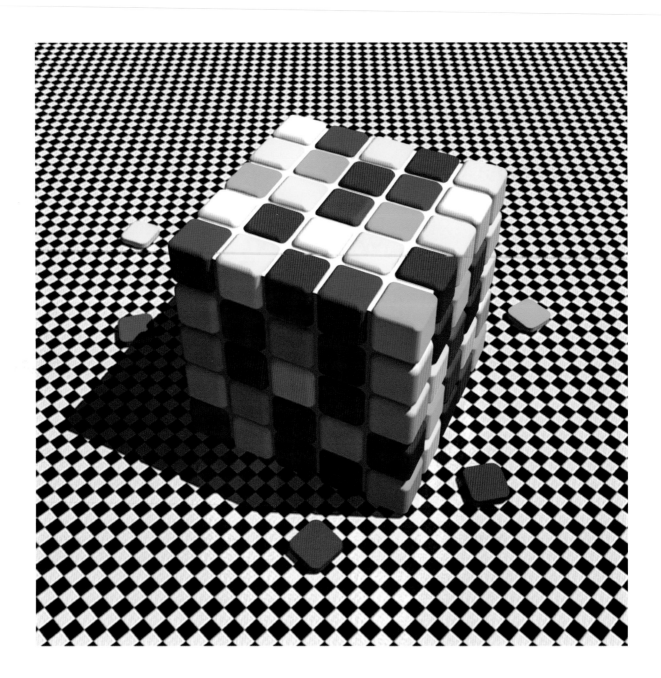

Purves and Lotto's Rubik's Cube Colour Illusion

Does the 'brown' square on the top of the Rubik's cube appear to be identical in colour to the 'yellow' square that is in the middle of the side within the shadow? They sure don't appear to be identical in colour, yet haven't we fooled you so far?

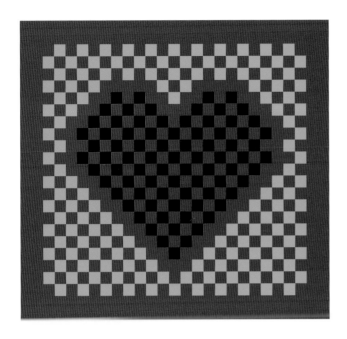

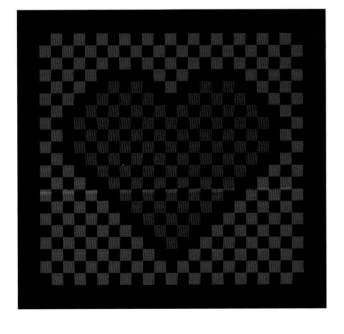

Chromostereopsis

Look at the different hearts. Which heart appears to float above the background, and which heart appears to sink to a lower level? If you move your head or the image, you might also notice that they appear to move.

Kitaoka's Ascending Dragons

The red is homogeneous over the figure, but appears to be red-purple behind blue lines or to be orange behind yellow lines.

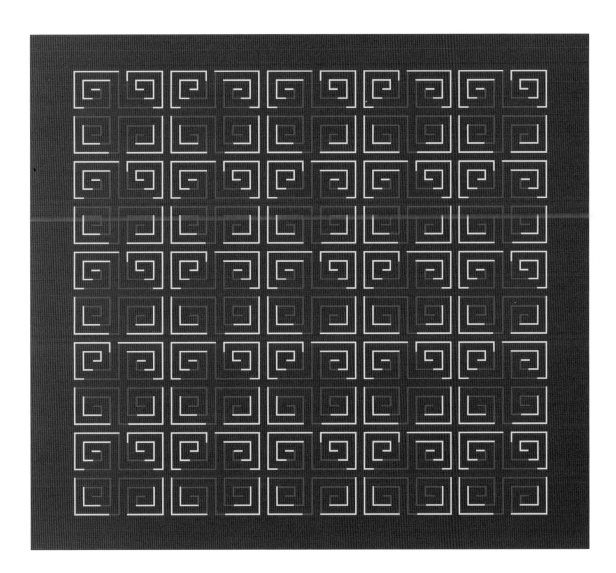

A Chinese Pattern and Colour Assimilation

The red appears to be magenta behind the blue lines while the same red appears to be orange behind the yellow lines.

Kitaoka's Bamboos of Sagano

The light green and dark green shown in oblique lines are identical to each other. The figure appears to tilt clockwise.

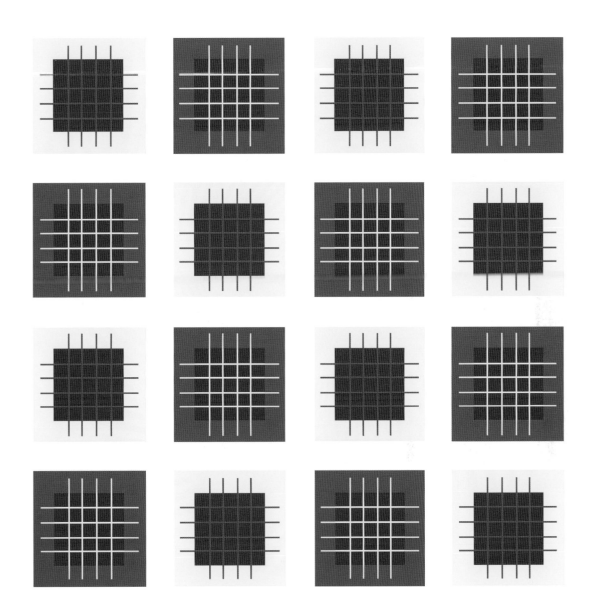

Chromatic Colour Assimilation

Red appears to be magenta or orange.

Kitaoka's Red Spiral

Red appears to be orange or magenta.

Colour Assimilation

The red squares on the yellow background appear different to those on the blue background. Such a phenomenon is called colour assimilation. This is the opposite of colour contrast, and there are black and white versions to be found in chapter one; however, the colour assimilation illusions are a bit more complex due to colour mechanisms. While the physiological mechanisms for brightness and colour contrast phenomena are well understood, how and when the assimilation occurs is not.

Neon Colour Spreading

The illusory square on the left appears to have a faint bluish colour even though there is no colour present. The region is completely white. This illusion is known as neon-colour spreading. The vertices form the edges of a surface. The visual system tends to spread colour within a bounded surface. On the right, when circles are placed at the edges of the illusory square, the neon colour spreading disappears. English vision scientist Marc Albert created this demonstration.

Pinna's Watercolour Effect

The large regions within the bordered area have no colour. The watercolour effect, recently discovered by Italian vision scientist Baingio Pinna, is elicited when a purple contour is accompanied by an orange inner edge. Under these conditions the entire enclosed area will appear to be uniformly coloured in the hue of the edge. The coloured flanking line accompanying the darker border assimilates its colour on to the enclosed white area over distances of up to 45°. The colour spreading is stronger on a white background than on grey or black backgrounds. The illusion is broken when a narrow white zone or gap is inserted in between the two inducing lines. It is not necessary, however, for the coloured lines to be continuous. Chains of coloured dots will also create the colour spreading illusion.

Purves and Lotto's Rubik's Cube Colour Illusion

Unbelievable as it seems, the 'brown' square on the top of the Rubik's cube is identical in colour with the 'yellow' square that is in the middle of the cube's side within the shadow. You can test this by covering everything except those two squares, and then when compared, you will see that they are identical. This may be one of the most powerful colour illusions known. Duke University neuroscientists Dale Purves and R. Beau Lotto have used this new illusion to show that colour perception can also be based on context and past experience. If you change the empirical meaning of the scene, for example, by removing the shadows, you not only change the brightness that people perceive, but also the colours as well.

Chromostereopsis

For more than half the number of observers, the black heart appears to float in front of the surround. However, some observers see the reversal. In this version, the heart appears to move frequently. For more than half of the observers, the red heart appears to float in front of the blue surround (upper panel) while the blue heart appears to sink behind the red surround (lower panel). However, some observers see the reversal. This demonstration depends on chromostereopsis. In addition, the hearts sometimes appear to move. Japanese vision scientist Akiyoshi Kitaoka created these examples.

Kitaoka's Ascending Dragons

This is an example of colour assimilation. Japanese vision scientist Akiyoshi Kitaoka created this figure.

A Chinese Pattern and Colour Assimilation

This is another example of colour assimilation by Japanese vision scientist Akiyoshi Kitaoka.

Chromatic Colour Assimilation

This is an example of colour assimilation. Japanese vision scientist Akiyoshi Kitaoka created this figure.

*T*his type of illusion has enjoyed greater popularity than any other. Popularly known as 'The Magic Eye', stereo illusion suggests a picture in depth. Many stereo illusions can trace their origins to the discovery of stereograms by the English scientist Charles Wheatstone, in 1838. Wheatstone showed that the retinal images from two independent sources could be fused into a single image, giving the immediate impression of depth. The effect was due to the difference of the images, not their similarity. Wheatstone further noticed that the views from the two eyes were different, hiding some objects and revealing others.

If you successively open only your right eye and then your left eye, you will see different views. All animals possessing overlapping optical fields have some depth perception. Even single dots can excite stereopsis, if there is some way for the mind to deduce correspondence. If the two images are too different, however, they cannot be fused into a single image of depth. They become instead alternating images, which the brain cannot decide upon. Stereopsis is the most reliable and the most important visual cue for processing depth information.

All stereo pictures are designed so that they can be seen if the viewer uses what is called the divergence method. In other words, your eyes must behave as if they are looking at something in the distance. Sometimes two dots are added to the top of the image as a helpful guide. If you focus correctly the two dots will become three dots. Remember, you must look at the image(s) long enough for your brain to resolve the stereo information. About 10 percent of people are stereo blind, and therefore cannot see this type of illusion.

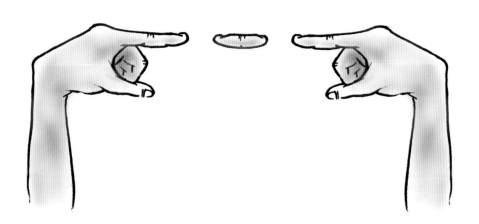

An Extra Finger

You can make a finger float right before your eyes in this fun illusion. Hold your two hands in front of your face at eye level. Keep the tips of your index fingers also at eye level. Focus on a wall several feet behind your fingers. You should see a finger float. Try moving your fingers closer to your face. What happens? If you focus on your fingers, instead of the wall, the illusion vanishes.

A Hole in Your Hand

Create a hole in your hand. Hold a tube up to your eye. Look at something 15 feet away with both eyes (one eye should look through the tube). Then bring your free hand up in front of the eye that is not looking through the tube. You will see the object through a round hole in the palm of your hand. For an interesting variation, place a coin in the centre of your palm and it will appear to float.

The Three Line Illusion

Hold the illustration so that it is just below both eyes and the image lies flat and perpendicular to your face. Look at the two lines with both eyes and after a while a third line will appear to rise out of the page.

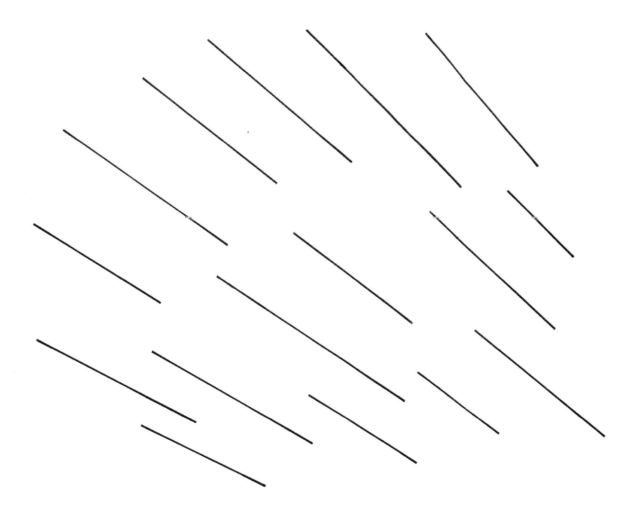

The Rising Lines Illusion

Can you make these lines rise out of the page? Tilt the page and look at the image with one eye from the bottom right side of the page.

An Antique Stereo View

Fuse these two images and you will see the scene in 3D.

A Picture in Stereo

Fuse these two images and you will see the scene in 3D.

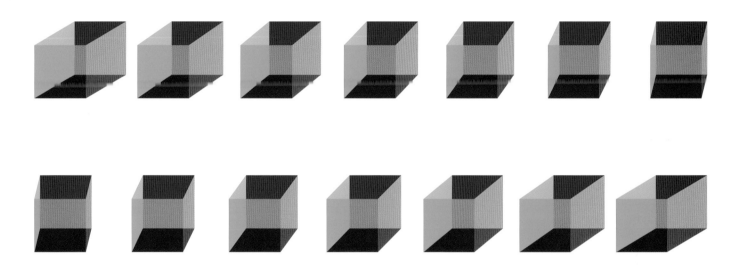

Kitaoka's Stereo Cubes

Free fuse this image and the cubes will appear to come out of the page. They can also be reversed.

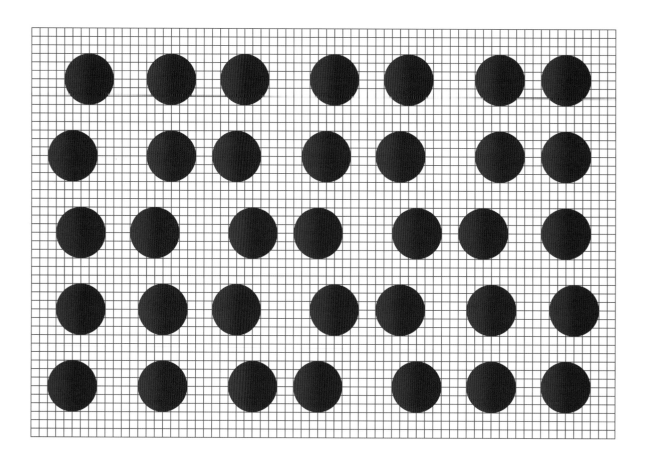

Balls at Many Different Levels

The depth of the mesh tends to be flush with the depth of the circle at which observers fixate.

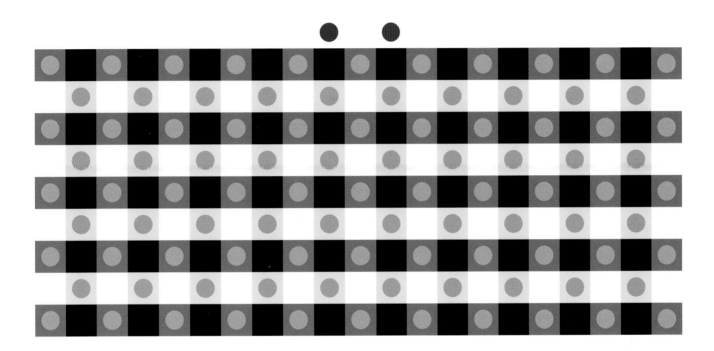

Snow at Many Different Depths

Free fuse this image. It looks like snow falling down to the right. In addition, grey circles appear to be of two different levels of lightness but they are identical in lightness.

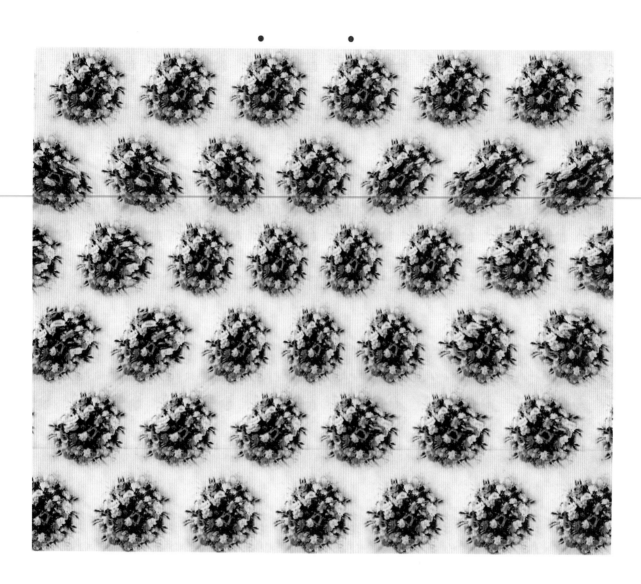

Stereogram

Free fuse this image. What is the hidden pattern that emerges?

The Wallpaper Illusion

Free fuse this image and it will appear in depth.

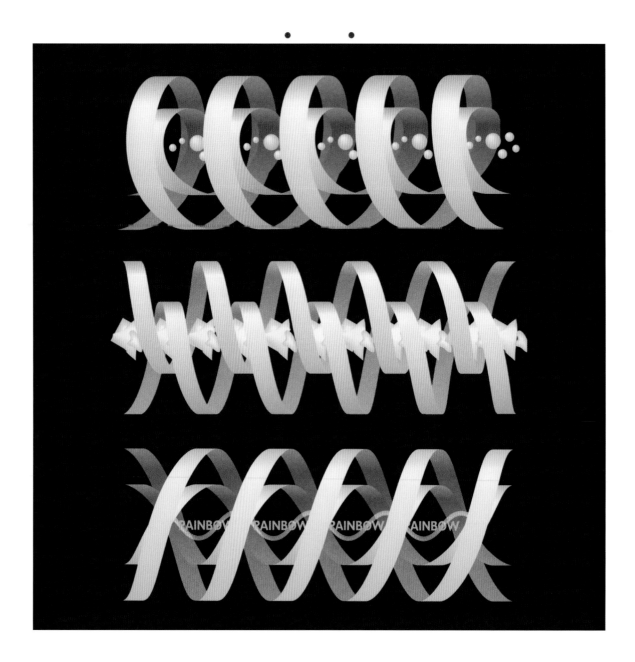

Another Wallpaper Illusion

Free fuse this image and it will appear in depth.

An Extra Finger

While you are focusing on the wall, the two fingers in the foreground incorrectly overlap when the images from both eyes are automatically combined. These overlapping images produce a stereogram with the floating finger.

A Hole in Your Hand

Your visual system fuses the images from both eyes creating the hole in the hand.

The Three Line Illusion

This particular viewpoint causes the images in each eye to fuse together, resulting in a third line that appears in stereo.

The Rising Lines Illusion

In the absence of stereo information, perceived depth and three-dimensional layout is determined by pictorial cues. In this case, the pictorial depth cues are ambiguous and the lines can be interpreted as both lying flat or rising above the page. The famous American psychologist William James discovered this illusion in 1908.

An Antique Stereo View

Stereo pictures were all the rage in the late nineteenth century, and were the first popular optical illusion fad to sweep country after country. Thousands of picturesque images were taken and mass-produced, and expensive stereo viewers were a sign of status.

Kitaoka's Stereo Cubes

Japanese vision scientist and 'Op' artist Akiyoshi Kitaoka created this stereo image.

Balls at Many Different Levels

Akiyoshi Kitaoka created this stereo image.

Snow at Many Different Depths

Akiyoshi Kitaoka created this stereo image.

Stereogram

A heart appears.

Most objects don't move. The ones that do, we need to be aware of so that we can act accordingly. Our visual perceptual system has evolved a complex process for the detection of motion. Most of the time, our eyes, head, and body are in motion, which makes it very difficult to equate object motion directly with image motion. It is also overly simplistic to think that all one has to do is process a change of an object's position over a period of time. Some objects move too quickly (such as fast moving bicycle wheel spokes), and others move too slowly (such as the planets and stars). Indeed, we can perceive motion when there is no motion, as in a movie, for example; we have a very vivid sensation of watching moving objects, but what is physically appearing on the screen is a rapid succession of still images.

Over the years, there have been various 'Op' artists who have instinctively created works of art that have stimulated a number of visual areas in the brain specifically concerned with visual motion. They convey (not suggest) actual motion where there is no motion.

Recently, a new class of relative motion illusions has been created, most notably by Baingio Pinna and Akiyoshi Kitaoka. Some of these illusions rely on either moving the image or the head to cause a perceived movement of the figure in a direction that is different from the one generated. With other images, even though both the head and the image may be steady, eye movements alone may induce the effect of relative motion. Despite the existence of a number of successful examples, there are still conflicting theories of why these illusions occur.

The Concentric Circles Illusion

Move this image in a circular fashion and the bicycle spokes will appear to turn.

MacKay's Figure of Eight Illusion

Move this figure either right or left and you will perceive blurred 'figures of eight' moving perpendicular to the true direction of motion. If you stare steadily at the centre you should see a rotation pattern. You can get the direction of rotation to change by fixating on a point left or right of the centre of the image.

Leviant's Enigma

Stare at the very centre of this image. Do you see motion in the blue rings? In what direction are they travelling? Do they change direction? How does the direction of motion in one ring relate to the direction of motion in another ring?

Waves

Move your eyes across this image, and you should see a powerful illusory depth motion.

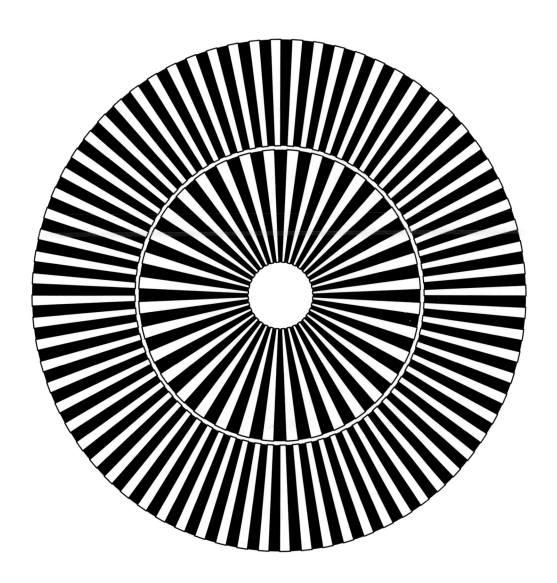

The Hula Hoop Illusion

View this image while moving it quickly in a circular fashion without changing its orientation. The motion should be similar to how you rinse a cup. You should see the intermediate circle move along with this movement, like a hoop being spun slowly around the hips.

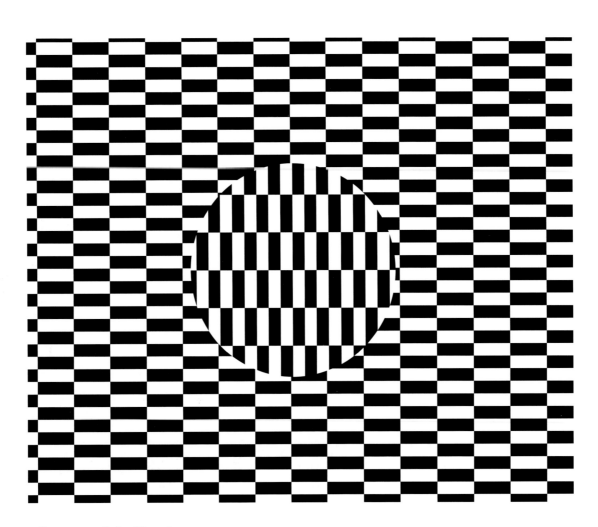

The Ouchi Illusion

If you move your eyes across this image or slowly shake the image, the centre section will appear to separate in depth and move slightly in a direction opposite to its surround.

Out of Focus

If you move your eyes across this image or slowly shake the image, the inset will appear to fluctuate.

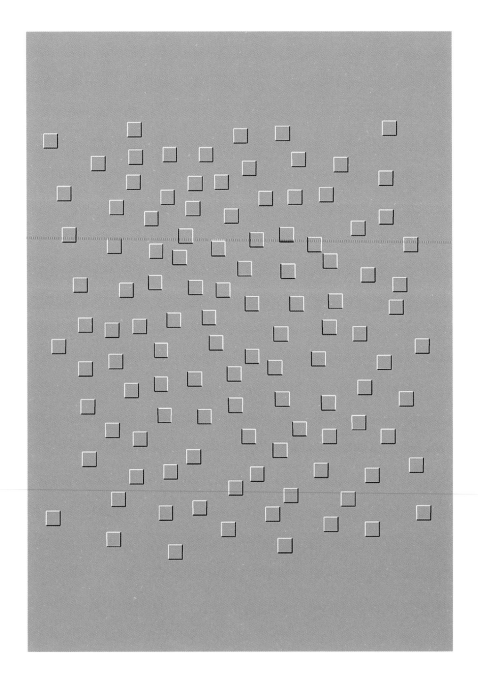

Pinna's Separating Squares Illusion

If you move your eyes across this image or slowly shake the image, the randomly placed centre squares will appear to separate in depth and move slightly differently to their surrounding squares.

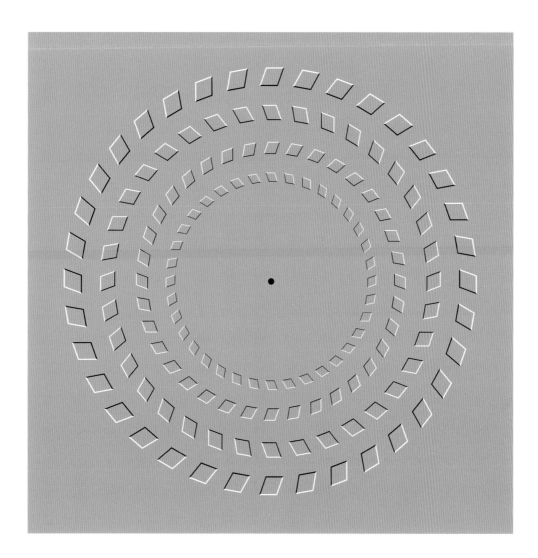

The Pinna-Brelstaff Revolving Circles Illusion

Stare at the centre of the image and slowly move your head towards the page, and then away from it. The circles should counter-rotate. When you move your head away from the page, both motions reverse direction, reversing the direction of the illusion.

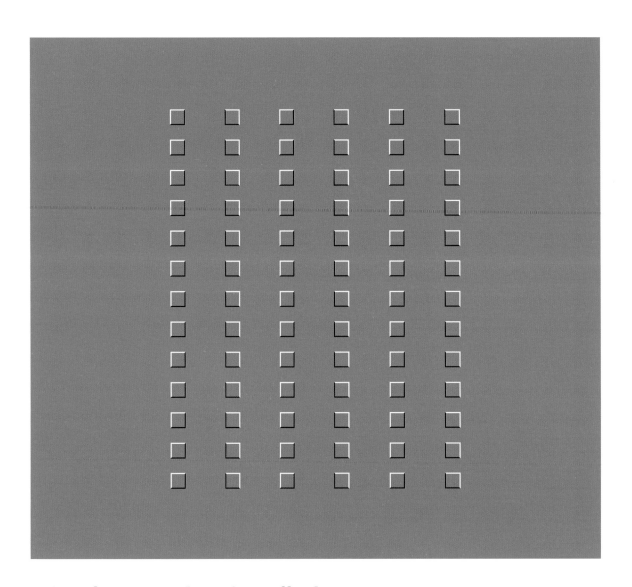

Pinna's Separating Lines Illusion

If you move this figure up and down the illusory motion is left and right.
If you move the sheet left and right, the illusory motion is up and down.

Kitaoka's Spinning Vortex Illusion

Move your head towards and away from this image, and it should slowly rotate.

Reginald Neal's Square of Three

This pattern appears to pulse and ripple as you stare at it.

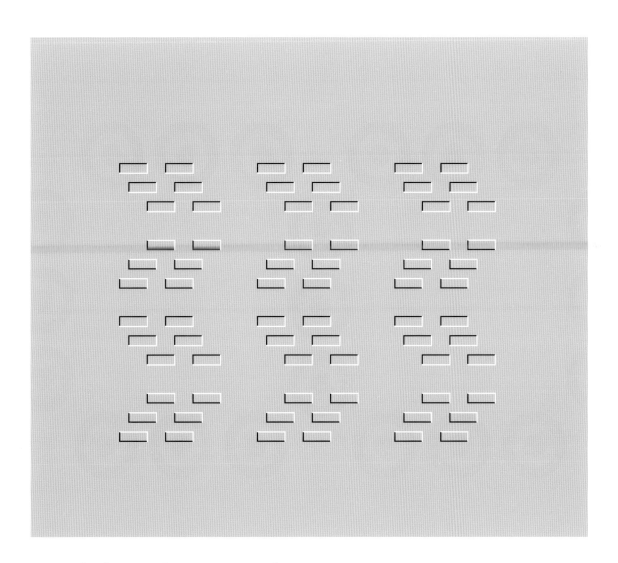

Kitaoka's Moving Rectangles

Move your head or the image and the rectangles will appear to move.

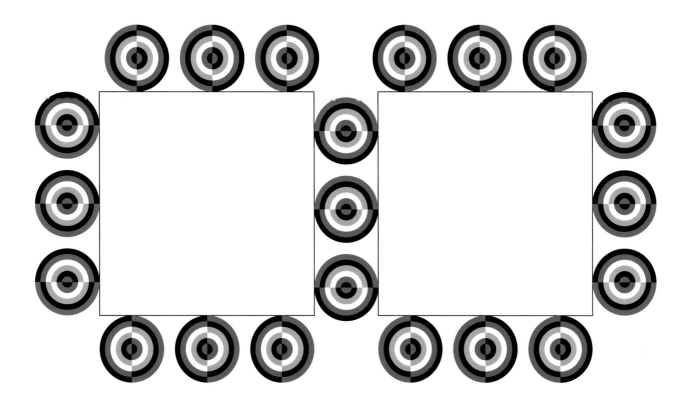

Convection

You do not have to move either your head or the image to make this illusion work. Just stare at the image and the round wheels will appear to move slowly around the squares. This illusion works best when seen through peripheral vision.

Kitaoka's Spinning Wheel Illusion

You do not have to move either your head or the image to make this illusion work. Just stare at the image and each circle will appear to rotate. In addition, concentric circles appear to be a spiral. This illusion works best when seen through peripheral vision.

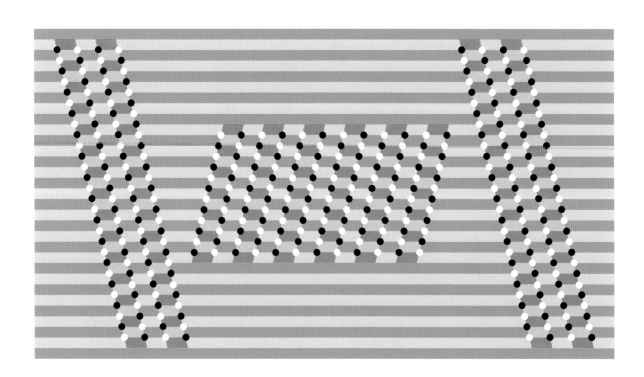

Ferry Boat

You do not have to move either your head or the image to make this illusion work. Just stare at the image and the slanted grey bars will appear to move in a horizontal direction. This illusion works best when seen through peripheral vision.

Kitaoka's Moving Lines

You do not have to move either your head or the image to make this illusion work. Just stare at the image and the horizontal lines will appear to move. This illusion works best when seen through peripheral vision.

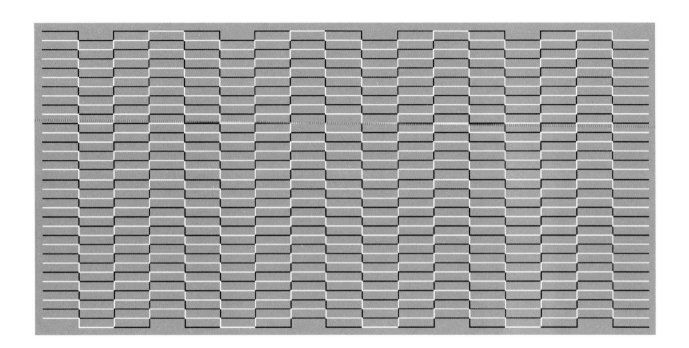

Kitaoka's Heat Devil

Stare at this image and it will appear to pulsate and fluctuate, very much like the movement of air that you see over a heated surface, known as a heat devil.

The Concentric Circles Illusion

This illusion, known as the Concentric Circles Illusion, was discovered by Charles Cobbold in 1881, and appeared in numerous advertising premiums in the late nineteenth and early twentieth centuries.

MacKay's Figure of Eight Illusion

This is known as MacKay's illusion, after it was first described in 1958 by Donald MacKay who noticed that light shining through horizontal venetian blinds will induce the appearance of vertical motion on an adjacent wall. It is not well understood why high-contrast thin lines produce motion effects perpendicular to the lines. There is currently an active controversy within the vision science community over the underlying mechanism that causes these effects.

Leviant's Enigma

Fixation on the centre induces in most, though not all, people a strong perception of motion occurring within the rings. The motion is in opposite directions in different rings and can change direction in any one ring during one, continuous, viewing. The streaming always moves perpendicular to the high contrast lines, which induce it. French artist Isia Leviant created this image in 1984, after being influenced by MacKay's illusions.

Waves

This is another example of high-contrast lines producing a powerful illusion of relative motion. In this case, you may also perceive a powerful illusory stereo illusion, and the waves may oscillate. English 'Op' artist Bridget Riley painted this work, 'Fall', in 1963.

The Hula Hoop Illusion

The Hula Hoop illusion was discovered by vision scientist Nicholas Wade.

The Ouchi Illusion

This illusion, first published in 1977 by Japanese 'Op' artist Hajime Ouchi, has been extensively researched and discussed by vision scientists due to its surprising illusory quality. Although the effect is still not fully understood, it is thought to relate to what is known as the 'aperture problem', which is how the visual system determines the direction of motion through an opening. Within that aperture, different physical motions are indistinguishable. For instance, a set of lines moving right to left produce the same spatio-temporal structure as a set of lines moving top to bottom. The aperture problem implies that motion sensitive neurons in the visual primary cortex will always respond to a contour that crosses their receptive field, independently of its true length and orientation, as long as its direction is consistent with the preferred direction of the neuron.

In the case of the Ouchi Illusion, it may be attributed to a bias in the way that local motion signals generated at different locations on each element are combined to code element motion. Integration of local motion signals is widely regarded as a necessary step in motion analysis to overcome the so-called aperture problem.

Out of Focus

Japanese vision scientist Akiyoshi Kitaoka created this variation of the Ouchi Illusion.

Pinna's Separating Squares Illusion

This is a new illusion created by Italian vision scientist Baingio Pinna. By moving the head back and forth or by moving the sheet in different directions, the randomly arranged elements appear to move in the opposite direction to the real motion, while at the same time producing a strong perception of depth segregation.

The Pinna-Brelstaff Revolving Circles Illusion

The rotation you perceive is called the Pinna-Brelstaff Revolving Circles Illusion, and is one of the most powerful illusory effects known. It is a recent discovery as it was first reported in 2000.

Italian vision scientist Baingio Pinna discovered that a certain class of flat static patterns will elucidate a strong illusory relative motion when moved across our visual field. The relative motion is always perpendicular to the true motion. Translatory, looming, and rotational movements of the head or the pattern can all elicit the effect. The effect is not due to head or eye movements, but to various orientation-selective cells found in the primary visual cortex, which get confused. These cells are responsible for detecting both the orientation and the direction of movement of lines and curves. Ordinarily, this works fine, but if the line is moving in any direction other than at a right angle to its orientation, the cells become confused. When you move your head or the image, the cells get confused, because the bars are moving in a perpendicular direction. When this happens, the two motions are added together, which creates an illusion of motion.

Pinna's Separating Lines Illusion

This is a variation of the Pinna-Brelstaff Revolving Circles Illusion discovered by Baingio Pinna in 2000.

Kitaoka's Spinning Vortex Illusion

This is a brand new illusion, discovered recently by Japanese vision scientist Akiyoshi Kitaoka. It is not fully understood what causes this effect, and there are several possible mechanisms at work. It is important that the dots have sharp edges for the effect to occur.

Reginald Neal's Square of Three

This is another example of high contrast thin lines causing an illusion. This illusion was created by American artist Reginald Neal.

Kitaoka's Moving Rectangles

This is Japanese vision scientist Akiyoshi Kitaoka's variation of one of Baingio Pinna's relative motion illusions.

Convection

This type of illusion is known as a peripheral drift illusion. It works best when seen through peripheral vision. If you fixate directly on the image, it will appear stationary. Eye movements may also be necessary to see the effect. Japanese vision scientist Akiyoshi Kitaoka created this version of the effect, which has been known since the 1970s. Kitaoka discovered that the order of the four coloured regions of different luminance, which have saw-tooth patterns, are critical to inducing the effect.

Kitaoka's Spinning Wheel Illusion

This is another example of a peripheral drift illusion by Japanese vision scientist Akiyoshi Kitaoka.

Ferry Boat

This is another variation of a peripheral drift illusion by Japanese vision scientist Akiyoshi Kitaoka. He titled this work 'Ferry Boat'.

Kitaoka's Moving Lines

This is another example of a peripheral drift illusion by Japanese vision scientist Akiyoshi Kitaoka.

Kitaoka's Heat Devil

It is not fully understood what gives rise to this effect, but eye movements certainly contribute to it. Japanese vision scientist Akiyoshi Kitaoka created it, and he titled this work 'Heat Devil'.

Impossible figures are a class of interesting two-dimensional perspective drawings that suggest three-dimensional physical objects with contradictory depth cues. Fun to look at and ponder, they can also reveal important insights into how we mentally construct three-dimensional percepts from two-dimensional images.

In these illusions, it is not the picture itself that is impossible, but your three-dimensional interpretation of it as a real physical object. A perspective drawing (possible or impossible) suggests a three-dimensional object, and your interpretation of it is highly constrained by how you interpret pictorial representations into three-dimensional mental percepts.

With an impossible figure, you must compare the different parts before you realize that it is impossible. However, as in many illusions, it is not always readily apparent that something is wrong. Initially, it may be that both your perception and your conception of the figure are fooled. Once you discover that your perception is being fooled, and you correct it, your visual system does not re-evaluate the impossible figure as a flat consistent/possible or misperceived object. You have encountered perceptual paradox.

This tendency for your visual system not to re-evaluate the image (based on actual knowledge) is true with all pictorial illusions where the meaning of the image is not ambiguous. Your correct conception of a pictorial illusion is not enough to override the constraints of your visual system. Your perceptions will continue to be fooled, although your conception will be fine.

The Fresco at Grote Kerk

Is there something wrong with this scene?

Hogarth's Mistakes of Perspective

How many perspective mistakes can you find in this image?

Reutersvärd's Impossible Triangle

This is a refined version by Oscar Reutersvärd of his original arrangement of cubes forming an impossible triangle.

How Many Prongs?

This is another classic impossible figure – the impossible fork. How many prongs can you count? Observe the whole length of the middle prong. What happens?

L'Egistential Elephant

Will this elephant have difficulty walking?

Escher's Belvedere

What is wrong with this structure?

Escher's Waterfall

Can water really flow like this?

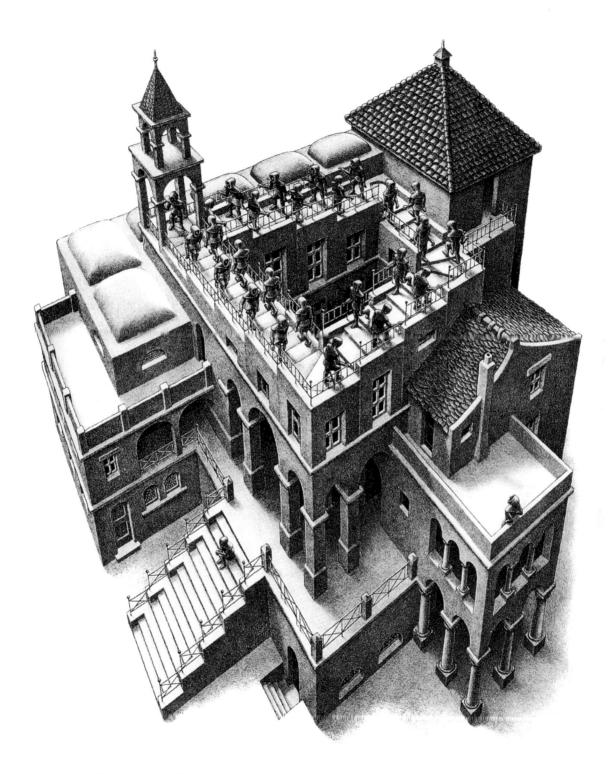

Ascending and Descending

Can you find the highest or lowest step?

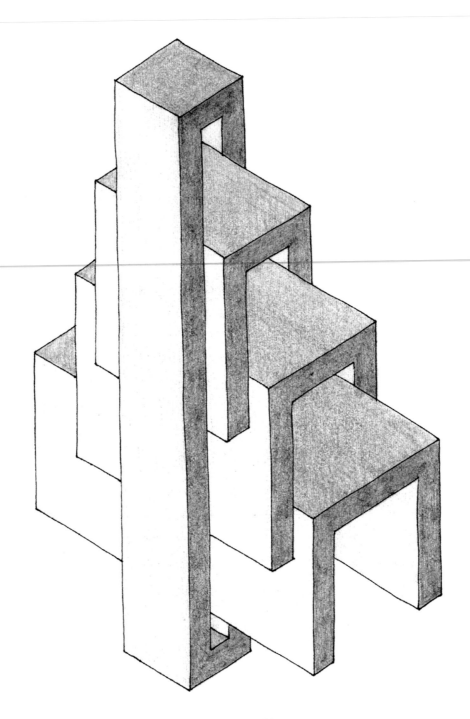

Larger Pieces Within Smaller Pieces

How can larger pieces fit within smaller pieces?

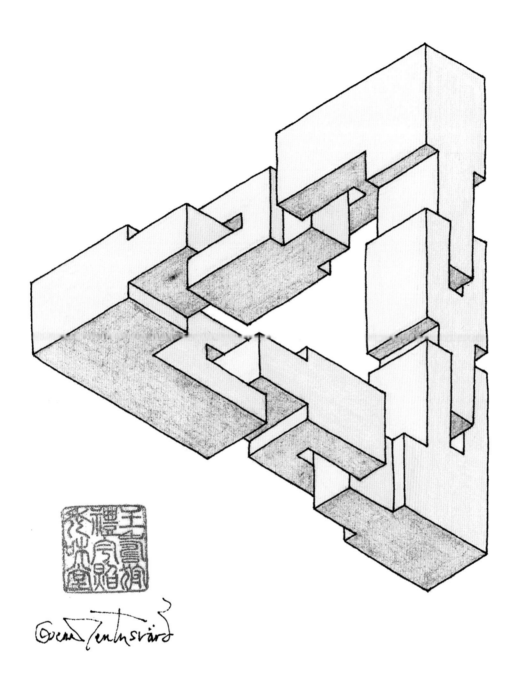

An Impossible Triangle with a Strange Twist

What is wrong with this figure?

An Impossible Staircase

What is impossible about this staircase?

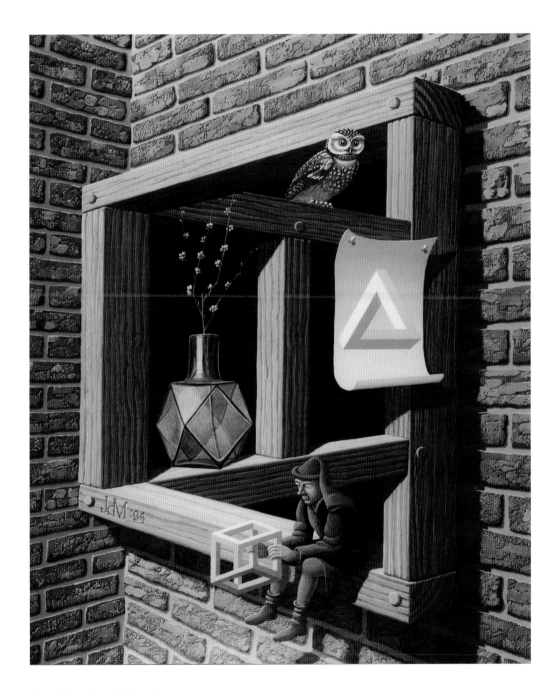

Unlikely Window!

This still life of a man sitting on a window ledge by Belgian artist Jos De Mey incorporates impossible triangles. The man holding the cube is in homage to the man holding an impossible cube in M.C. Escher's 'Belvedere'.

Melancholy Tunes on a Flemish Winter's Day

How does the left column come forward?

Between Illusion and Reality

What is peculiar about the two openings?

The Folded Chess Set

Are you looking at this chessboard from the bottom or the top? The ladders also twist in a strange way. Swiss artist Sandro Del Prete created this charming image. Compare this image with the one on the next page.

The Impossible Terrace

Are you seeing the balcony from the bottom or the top?

Peregrination

Is this an impossible building?

The Fresco at Grote Kerk

The medieval fresco found at Grote Kerk, Breda, Holland is typical of a perspective mistake that could be described as an impossible figure. The centre pillar is simultaneously on two different depth planes.

Hogarth's Mistakes of Perspective

In 1754, William Hogarth, in this now famous engraved frontispiece, made fun of artists who created perspective errors. Hogarth, by depicting the deliberate use of perspective, wanted to draw attention to the power of proper perspective.

How Many Prongs?

It is easy to describe the multiple sources of confusion in the impossible fork. First of all, the impossible fork lacks the intact borders characteristic of solid objects. The figure does not have a silhouette and cannot be coloured in. The outline of the middle prong merges into the outline of the two outer prongs. In addition, the middle prong appears to drop to a level lower than the two outer prongs. The figure is particularly unusual because it gives the initial impression of being an intact solid, when in fact it does not have a complete contour. Finally, you will notice that three prongs miraculously turn into two prongs. The paradox is quite powerful, because within it are various impossibility sources.

Cover the right half of the figure. The left half is perfectly possible. The foreground figure is perceived as built of flat faces constituting two rectangular prongs.

Now cover the left half and look only at the right half of the figure. You interpret this figure as curved surfaces constituting three separate cylindrical lines.

Locally this figure is fine, but globally it presents a paradox.

It is not known who first created this figure, although its first publication was in 1964, and it has been reprinted many times since.

L'Egistential Elephant

Stanford psychologist Roger Shepard created an interesting variation on the impossible fork in his depiction of an impossible elephant. To avoid the counting paradox with the number of legs, Shepard introduced the more conspicuous line discontinuity at the far right. Contrast this with

the impossible fork. Both of these figures have discontinuous boundaries, but the impossible fork exhibits no unclosed lines.

Escher's Belvedere

This is Dutch graphic artist M.C. Escher's first impossible print, created in 1958, and is entitled 'Belvedere'. The top floor is perpendicular to the bottom floor. The sitting man is holding an impossible cube.

Escher's Waterfall

M.C. Escher's famous print 'Waterfall', created in 1961, was inspired by Roger Penrose's impossible triangle. Escher actually used three impossible triangles joined together to form the basis of the structure. During preparatory sketches for this print, Escher's original intention was to draw three colossal building complexes. However, while working, Escher realized that falling water could be used to illustrate the impossible triangle in a unique way. The water spills over an edge and draws a wheel. The water then flows away from the wheel through a brick channel. If you follow the course of the water you will see that it flows downward and into the dirt until it again reaches the furthest and lowest point, which is identical with its highest and nearest point. Therefore, the water is able to fall again and keep the wheel turning.

Ascending and Descending

This 1961 work, entitled 'Ascending and Descending' by M.C. Escher is based on Lionel Penrose's impossible staircase. If you follow the steps around, you will not locate either the lowest or highest step. The figures on the steps are monks. Escher drew the staircase in perspective, which would indicate another size illusion. The monks that are descending should get smaller, and the ones that are ascending should get larger. They don't. Although, Escher was very exact in his perspective, in this case, he was prepared to cheat a little bit.

Larger Pieces Within Smaller Pieces

Swedish artist Oscar Reutersvärd created a new depth paradox. The drawing appears to suggest that larger pieces are fitting within smaller pieces.

An Impossible Triangle with a Strange Twist

Look at the top portion of the two bars. One bar

passes behind and merges with the other bar in an impossible way. A line normally cannot change its interpretation from convex (as when two surfaces meet away from the viewer) to concave (when two surfaces meet pointing towards the viewer), or vice versa, without passing through a vertex. The upper portion of the lighter coloured surface ends in a Y vertex on its right side, with the middle segment being concave. As that segment extends upward towards the red cube, it becomes convex without passing through a vertex, clearly an impossibility.

An Impossible Staircase

Every step is level with the surrounding plane.

Melancholy Tunes on a Flemish Winter's Day

This illusion of a multiplane impossibility is very similar to the one created unintentionally in the medieval fresco at Grote Kerk. Nevertheless, the basis of this illusion is the impossible triangle, which is very cleverly concealed by Belgian artist Jos De Mey.

Between Illusion and Reality

The physical construction of this scene is impossible. Carefully examine the two passages by first covering the bottom half. You will notice that the top half of the passage extends outward. This is perfectly possible. If you then cover the top half of the passage, you will see that the bottom passage extends inward, which is physically incompatible with the protruding top section. The critical transition occurs at about the upper quarter of the panel with the faint people on the left. That quarter is opaque, but the lower portion appears open. This would almost never occur in natural scenes without a definite boundary between the two.

The Impossible Terrace

Graphic artist David MacDonald adapted Del Prete's 'Folded Chess Set' into an impossible balcony. It is interesting to compare the two images. Note that MacDonald had difficulty successfully resolving the two different perspectives created by adding the balcony balusters. He had to literally chop off the right and left ends of the image to make this image work. Del Prete's image was more successful in this regard.

Our visual environment is filled with shadows cast by objects, both in daylight and under artificial illumination. Shadows may be faint or diffuse, but they are almost always there. Artists appreciate the importance of shadow in trying to suggest a realistic three-dimensional scene. If shadows are not depicted correctly, the balance of a work of art can be seriously affected and a wrong or inappropriate impression conveyed. Although you may not be paying conscious attention to them, they are playing an active role in your mental construction of your environment.

Part of visual perception involves the interpretation of visual scenes based on generalities from our environment. The direction of light and shadow involves certain regularities that are exploited by our perceptual system. For example, light and illumination usually comes from above. Illumination from above can cause regularities with regard to shadows and shading in areas of depth. Your visual system interprets these regularities to help determine shape and depth.

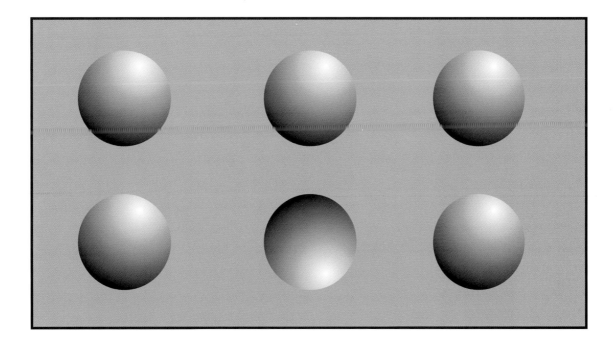

Shape from Shading

How many areas are concave? How many are convex? Turn the image upside-down and count again.

Concave or Convex?

There are quite a number of depressions in the plaster, but what happens to these depressions when you turn the image upside down?

Can You Find the Deer?

There is a deer hiding here. To find him, turn the page upside down and look at it from a distance. You should see the deer 'pop' out.

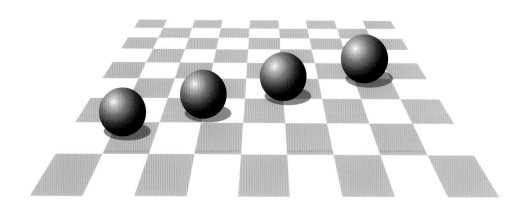

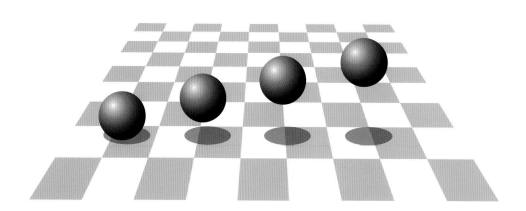

Kersten's Ball and Shadow Illusion

Are the balls in the two illustrations in different positions relative to the background?

The Mysterious Floating Vase

Does this vase appear to be floating off the ground?

Which is Real?

Compare the two photographs of the same mountain scene. One of these images is the normal photograph, while the other is its negative. Which is which? What clues provide the answer?

A Cat Hiding in Its Own Shadow

Which is the cat and which is the shadow of a cat? Is the black cat walking on a grey pavement or on the grass?

Mary Poppins and Her Shadow

Can you see the shadow of Mary Poppins?

Motorcycle and Shadow

Japanese artist Shigeo Fukuda arranged forks, knives, and spoons, to case a shadow of a motorcycle.

Concave or Convex?

They become convex. Your brain uses clues to determine depth from a two-dimensional image. One clue is shading. In this illusion, the shading is ambiguous. Thus, depending on where your brain perceives the light as coming from, the shading will dictate whether the bulges are perceived as concave or convex. Normally, light comes from above. When the image is inverted, the light and shading is reversed. This wonderful shape from shading illusion was created by noted American children's author and photographer Walter Wick.

Can You Find the Deer?

Turn the image upside down and look at it from a distance. This is a wonderful design involving shape and shading by noted American children's author and photographer Walter Wick.

Kersten's Ball and Shadow Illusion

In the top illustration, the balls appear to be resting on the surface and receding into the distance. In the bottom illustration, the balls appear to be rising above the surface and not receding. The only difference between the two illustrations is the placement of the cast shadows, which provide a context for interpreting the three-dimensional position of the ball relative to the background. Without a shadow the position of the balls is ambiguous. Vision scientists Dan Kersten and David Knill first described this effect in 1996.

The Mysterious Floating Vase

The vase is resting on the ground. As in the previous example, shadow is a very important cue for your interpretation of position of an object relative to its background. In this case, special lighting techniques were used to separate the shadow from the object, so that it gives the impression that it is in fact floating.

Which is Real?

Many people incorrectly believe that the mountain with the snow is the real image. In fact, it is the negative. What people believe is snow is actually the shadows of the mountain. Photo B is the positive. Harvard vision scientist Patrick Cavanagh created this demonstration.

A Cat Hiding in Its Own Shadow

The intersection between the grey wall or pavement and the grass is ambiguous, so it is difficult to tell whether the grey area is a vertical wall or pavement. Hence, it is confusing to determine whether the cat's shadow is on the grass or on the wall. However, there are a variety of small cues, such as two ears on the cat, one ear on the shadow, that do give away the fact that the cat is walking on the grey pavement. Joe Burull captured this interesting scene.

Mary Poppins and Her Shadow

A shadow sculpture by Japanese artist Shigeo Fukuda.

Your visual system needs to establish the location of objects in the world accurately, not only for navigation, but also for grasping and for determining the distance of predators. Perceiving depth is a fundamental visual task, and your visual perceptual system has evolved a variety of ways to determine the size and distance relationship between objects of differing distances.

Stereo information (binocular vision), convergence (the turning in of our eyes as objects come close to us), accommodation (the change of focus that occurs when the lens of the eye changes size), contrast, colour and brightness are all cues which provide us with distance and size information.

The most obvious method your visual system has evolved to determine size-distance relationships is, however, perspective, where lines radiate to some common point in the distance. Perspective was discovered and developed in the early fifteenth century through the pioneering work of Filippo Brunelleschi and Leon Battista Alberti. Their methods transformed Western art, which became more natural and realistic as a result.

A realistic three-dimensional scene in art is an illusion. Yet, these same perspective rules discovered by artists can also be used to create illusions that suggest scenes in perspective that are not consistent with their physical reality.

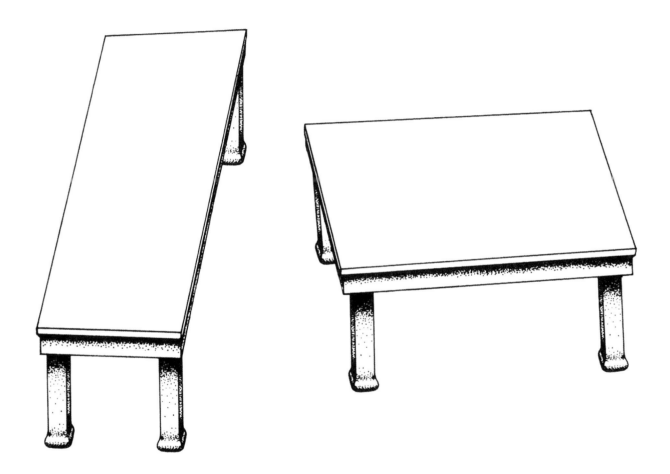

Shepard's Tabletop Illusion

These two tabletops are exactly identical in size and shape.
If you don't believe it, trace them out and compare.

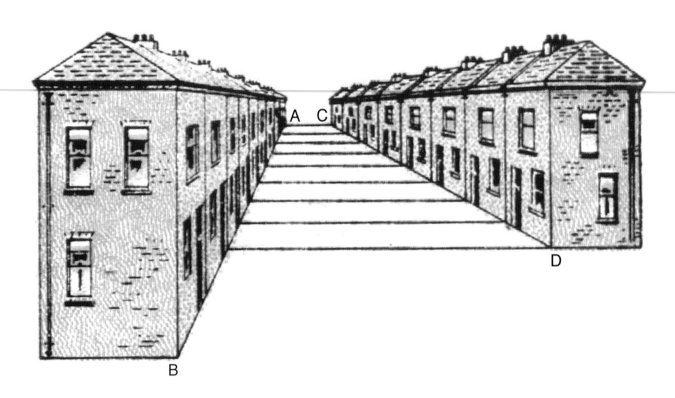

An Illusion of Extent

Although they appear to be dramatically different in length, lines AB and CD are equal.

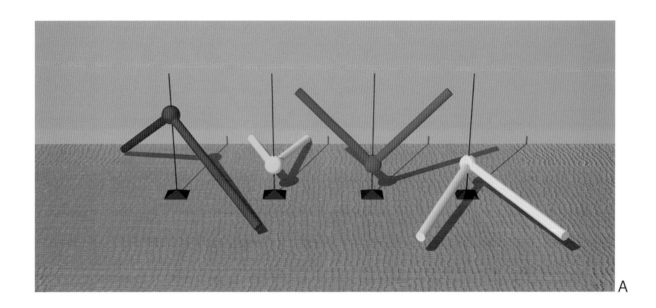

Do You Have the Right Angle?

Photo A. Without using a measuring device, which angle appears the largest? Which angle appears the smallest? Arrange the angles in order of descending order of angular size.

Photo B: Do all the angles appear to be the same size?

Terra Subterranea

Does the background figure appear to be larger than the foreground figure? It would appear to be that way, yet they are both identical in size.

144

The Hallway Illusion

This scene looks perfectly natural, except for the man in the lower right-hand corner, who appears to be a midget. Yet, he is identical in size to the figure in the background.

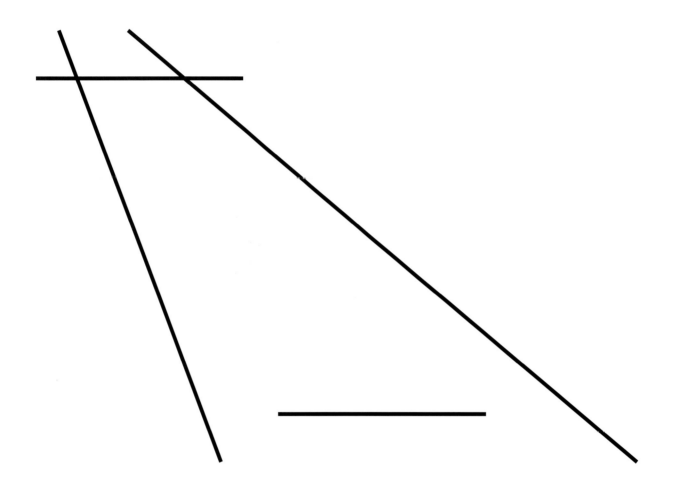

The Ponzo Illusion

Which horizontal line is longer?

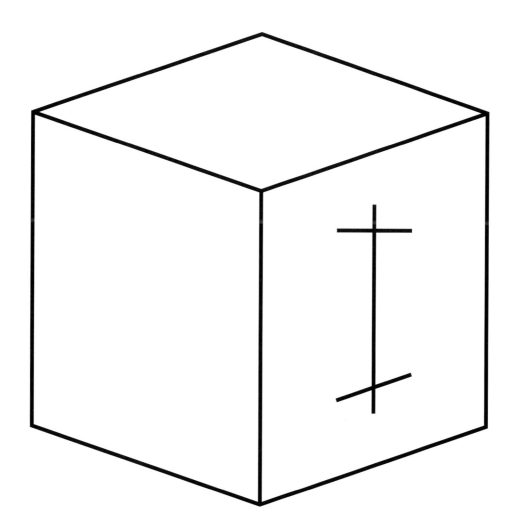

The Perspective Box Illusion

Look at the figure on the outside of the cube. Which line is perpendicular to the vertical line and which line is at an angle? Cover just the outline of the cube and you will see your perception change.

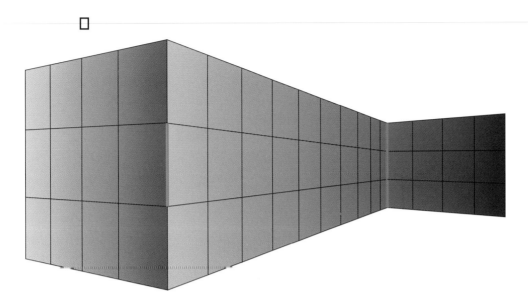

The Müller-Lyer Illusion in Perspective

Which red line is longer?

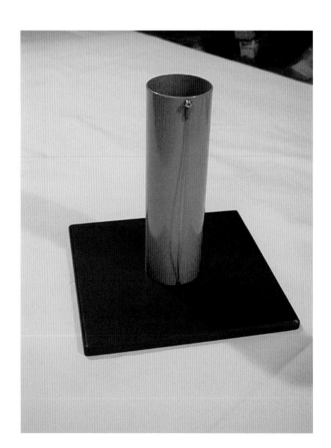

A Foreshortening Illusion

Visually estimate, but do not mathematically calculate, the circumference of the cylinder's rim. Would you say that your estimate is less than, equal to, or more than the height of the cylinder?

Shepard's Tabletop Illusion

Although the drawing is flat, it suggests a three-dimensional object. The table's edges and legs provide perspective cues that influence your interpretation of its three-dimensional shape and constancy. This powerful illusion clearly demonstrates that your brain does not take a literal interpretation of what it sees. Stanford psychologist Roger Shepard created this tabletop illusion.

An Illusion of Extent

Again, perspective cues provide a three-dimensional context for perceiving length.

Do You Have the Right Angle?

In the top photo, although it is hard to believe, all the coloured angles are right angles. An image of an angle on the retina is quite ambiguous. We need to know its precise angle in depth. According to Dale Purves and R. Beau Lotto of Duke University, the orientation of the angle exerts a strong bias in the judgement of its extent, depending on the frequency of occurrence of particular angles at that orientation in our experience. Angles at the orientation of the red angle tend to be large and those at the green angle tend to be small, so we overestimate the red as large and we underestimate the green.

In the bottom photo, although the angles all appear to be identical, they are in fact, quite dissimilar. So, it is quite possible to make physically different angles appear the same by presenting mutually inconsistent information. Although each of these objects appears to form a right angle, none of them projects in this way.

This illusion is greatly weakened for people who have extensive experience in building carpentered works.

Terra Subterranea

This drawing by Stanford psychologist Roger Shepard suggests a three-dimensional scene in perspective. This illustration is a good example of how your brain interprets images.

Normally, two things happen when objects recede into the distance. First, the visual angle of the receding object gets smaller. This should be familiar to you. Far away objects appear smaller. Secondly, the further an object moves away from you, the closer it approaches a visual horizon. This is consistent with how we draw pictures in perspective. When we see a normal object receding away from us, its visual angle shrinks and it approaches a visual horizon.

In Shepard's drawing, however, the background figure has approached a visual horizon, but its visual angle has not correspondingly decreased. If the two figures were identical in size, and one was in the background, it should have a smaller visual angle. However, in this case, the figure in the background has the same visual angle as the figure in the foreground. Therefore, your visual/perceptual system interprets the background figure as larger than the foreground figure. This drawing shows in a very vivid way that the brain is a great interpreter! If you could move the background figure down to the same horizon level as the foreground figure, the illusion would disappear.

The Hallway Illusion

This illusion, known as the Hallway Illusion, is similar to the previous example, except that the figure on the lower right is on the same horizon line as the larger foreground figure, but now the visual angle is smaller, but it has not approached a visual horizon. Therefore, the figure is consistent with a figure that is smaller, not one that has receded into the distance. This illusion is the basis of the well-known size illusion that takes place in the Ames Room; an example can be seen in the chapter on architectural illusions.

The Ponzo Illusion

The two horizontal lines are identical in size. The converging lines provide important perspective cues. Italian vision scientist Mario Ponzo discovered this classic illusion in 1914.

The Perspective Box Illusion

The perspective cues of the box provide a context for the orientation of the line segments of the central figure. Remove the perspective cues from the box, and your visual system must use another context.

The Müller-Lyer Illusion in Perspective

They are both identical in length. Although the Müller-Lyer illusion is not a perspective illusion, it can be augmented through perspective cues, as in this example.

A Foreshortening Illusion

The height of the cylinder is equal to its circumference. Most people estimate that the circumference around the cylinder's rim is less than the vertical length of the cylinder. If you measured the rim with a string, and then held it beside the cylinder it would extend all the way down its length, which is consistent with elementary geometry ($C = 2\pi r$).

The illusion is due in part because the lip of the rim is foreshortened and the length of the rim is not foreshortened at all.

It is highly important for your visual perceptual system to ascribe meaning to a scene. This allows you to make sense of the world.

Normally, scenes do not have multiple meaningful interpretations – a single interpretation is clear. In figure/ground relationships the figure is usually the meaningful part of the image. Once your visual system has locked in a meaningful interpretation of a scene, it is very difficult, if not impossible, for it to overcome that interpretation. Throughout this book, you will encounter all sorts of illusions where you have no conscious control over your perceptions, either by successive experience or knowledge. One of few classes of illusion, which you have some perceptual control over, are images where the meaning of the image has been made deliberately ambiguous. These types of images have been popular for well over a hundred years, and there are examples dating back several hundred years.

When the meaning of the image is ambiguous, your visual perceptual system will flip-flop back and forth between the two interpretations. However, once your visual system has disambiguated figure from ground, and given the scene a meaningful interpretation, then you can never go back to its original meaningless interpretation again. It will not flip-flop.

One Head or Two?

Do you perceive one head or two profiles?

Can You Find Both the Old and Young Woman?
Can you find both the profile of an old woman and a young woman?

The Flowering of Love

Can you find the lovers in the flowers?

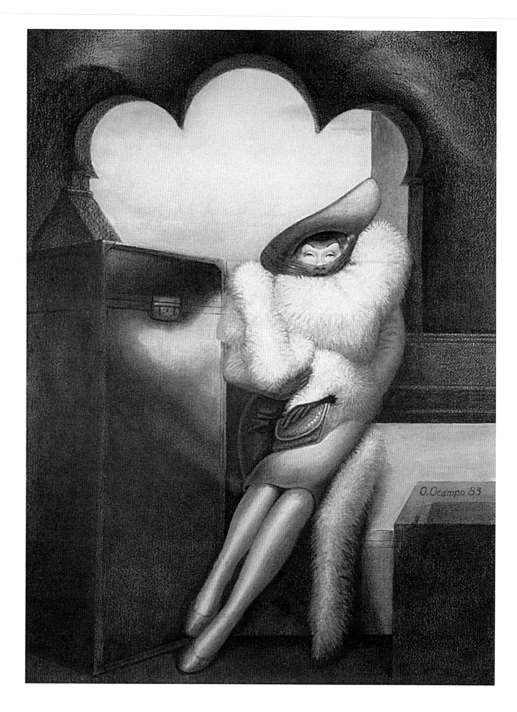

Marlene

Can you find the portrait of Marlene Dietrich?

A Strange Coincidence

What's going on here?

Angels

Can you find both the heads and bodies of angels?

The Mysterious Lips

Do you perceive the face?

Ten Bodies and Five Heads

How many bodies and heads can you count?

Visions of Don Quixote

How many hidden faces can you find?

Island for the Dogs

Is this island for the dogs?

In Search of a Missing Dog

What does this image represent?

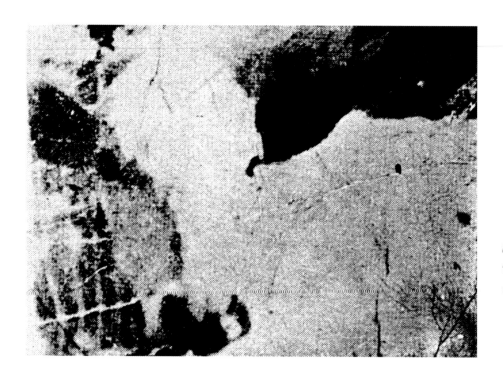

Find What Got Out of the Barn

What does this image represent?

Find the Missing Person

What does this image represent?

One Head or Two?

This is a very nice example of an ambiguous illustration that 'flip-flops' in meaning. It is possible to see a single face (front-on view) which is partially occluded by the candlestick. In this interpretation, you get a perception of depth because the candlestick is in front of the face. In the second interpretation, you will see the profiles of two women on either side of the candlestick. The contours that define each interpretation are ambiguous, which results in the two separate interpretations. Stanford psychologist Roger Shepard created this charming variation on Edgar Rubin's famous figure/ground face/vase illusion.

Can You Find Both the Old and Young Woman?

Both interpretations are possible. This classic illusion demonstrates how your visual system tends to group features based upon what you expect to see. If you perceive one feature as the eye, then the nose, mouth, and chin get grouped and identified accordingly.

The American psychologist Edwin Boring created the most famous version of this illusion in the 1940s, but its roots can be traced back to the late nineteenth century, when it first appeared on puzzle trading cards.

The Flowering of Love

The petals of the rose form the outline of a couple kissing or that of a single rose. The contours that define each interpretation are ambiguous, which results in the two separate interpretations. Swiss artist Sandro Del Prete created this ambiguous illusion.

Marlene

Mexican artist Octovio Ocampo created this charming scene of the famous 1940s film star.

A Strange Coincidence

Despite its contrived nature, children especially enjoy this illustration of a strange scene at a tavern by British illustrator Bush Hollyhead.

Angels

The heads contain the figure of the angel. Mexican artist Octovio Ocampo created this ambiguous scene.

The Mysterious Lips

The Spanish surrealist Salvador Dalí, who was fascinated by ambiguous imagery, entitled this scene, 'The Mysterious Lips that Appeared on the Back of My Nurse', which was painted in 1941.

Ten Bodies and Five Heads

There are five heads, but one can count ten full bodies. This type of illusion has been popular since the seventeenth century and examples can be found in both Western, Oriental, and Indian engravings, where one head belongs to two bodies.

Visions of Don Quixote

There are several faces hidden in this image, but the main scene is ambiguous with a portrait of Don Quixote. Mexican artist Octovio Ocampo closely based this illustration on an original ambiguous drawing of Don Quixote by Swiss artist Sandro Del Prete.

Island for the Dogs

You can perceive both an island and two dogs. Its origin is unknown, but it probably dates from the nineteenth century. It is entitled 'Isle of the Dogs'.

In Search of a Missing Dog

A Dalmatian dog. What normally constitutes figure and ground have been deliberately obscured, making it very difficult at first to discern the meaning of this image. However, your visual/perceptual system will try very hard to ascribe meaning to each image, and will engage in an active search until it arrives at a meaningful result.

Once you perceive the Dalmatian dog, for example, the picture becomes dramatically reorganized with certain parts of the dots being grouped with the dog and other dots with the background. This illustrates the importance of prior experience on visual perception, especially if the organization and meaning of the image is highly ambiguous.

Once you perceive the Dalmatian dog the meaningful interpretation dominates, and it is virtually impossible to see it again in its original meaningless interpretation. This is an example of a non-reversible figure/ground illusion.

Find What Got Out of the Barn

The head of a cow. The explanation for this effect is similar to the last example.

Find the Missing Person

A bearded man.

Psychologists have long known that context and expectation can influence perception. Now we know that context can dramatically influence your perception of a scene in many fundamental ways. Over the years, there have been numerous classic studies demonstrating how a person's perception of an event can be dramatically controlled through priming and context. This is why witness testimony has been so notoriously unreliable. It is well known that witnesses to a crime or sudden dramatic event will give wildly differing accounts of what happened.

It is also possible to 'prime' a person to influence their perception in a particular direction. Priming occurs when you hear or see a word, or an image, and you relate it to some other information. Studies have shown, for example, that many more people have reported seeing a UFO after watching a television programme about extra-terrestrial visits.

Priming is also related to the notion that suggestion can influence judgements. There is a whole marketing industry that tries to influence consumer decisions through subliminal advertising. Although we can describe the different accounts of perceptual priming, we have no understanding at any level of why these perceptions occur.

A Strange Catch

Cover the man and the fish appears to be a normal size. Cover the hand and the fish appears to be a remarkable catch.

The Loch Ness Monster?

This is a photograph purported to be the famous Loch Ness monster taken on Loch Ness. Do you think it is the monster?

Earthquake Zone

Does this bookcase appear to be falling?

What's This?

Can you make sense of this bizarre scene? The photograph has not been altered.

An Illusion for the Birds

On an island off the coast of Maine, in the USA, a puffin, left, stands among three decoy puffins placed there by the National Audubon Society, a conservation group. Because of over-hunting, puffins vanished in the 1800s from their island homes. Now people are trying to lure them back. It appears that the decoys are working. So, birds can be fooled by context too.

You See What?

What you perceive here is based upon past experience.

A Strange Flock

Is this really a flock of sheep?

171

Priming Illusion

This is a fun priming illusion to try out on your friends. Have your friend say the word 'white' out loud ten times. Make them then repeat the word again ten times, but this time really loud. When they are finished, ask them to quickly answer the question 'What does a cow drink?'

172

1000
20
30
1000
1030
1000
+   20
_____

? ? ? ?

It's a Matter of Counting

Add up the row of numbers out loud in groups. What is your answer? Do it again. Most people get the wrong answer! Try it on your friends for hilarious results. Only look at the correct answer after you have tried it.

Hysteresis

Here you see a series of images that transform from one interpretation (a man's head) to a different interpretation (a kneeling woman). Starting with the man's head, look at each image in sequence, and determine at which point your interpretation of the images switches over to that of a kneeling woman. Then start with the kneeling woman, and work your way back to the image of the man's head. Again, note at what point your interpretation of the image switches over to that of the man's head.

red   green

blue   orange

black blue

yellow **gray**

red   pink

Stroop Effect

In the list of coloured words above, don't say the word, say the colour of the word. Try to do this task as fast as you can. You will find it is not so easy.

A Strange Catch

A scene's context can influence your perception of relative size.

The Loch Ness Monster?

Illusions can often be formed by context and expectation. This floating log would never be mistaken for anything else, except from the shore of Loch Ness in Scotland. A tourist, waiting on the shore to see the elusive monster, took this picture, hoping that he at last had captured on film proof of the famous monster. No doubt the heading of this illusion also primed you.

Earthquake Zone

This bookcase built by the author, who lives in California, an area known for earthquakes, is based on a design by Ron Christenson. The placement of the leaning books is critical for the illusion.

What's This?

It is a dancer, whose hands are in the shoes and his head is tucked behind one of his arms. Although the parts of this image are easily identifiable, they are intentionally posed to present an overall configuration that does not conform to your normal experience. Therefore, your perceptual system when first presented with this scene has a hard time grouping the familiar parts into a coherent and meaningful representation. After looking at this image for a while, you do some perceptual problem solving so that the overall scene takes on a more meaningful and less bizarre interpretation. Once your perceptual system locks into a meaningful interpretation, it is almost impossible to perceive this image in any other way. This demonstrates the importance of meaning to image interpretation for your perceptual system.

You See What?

This is an excellent example of priming by experience. If you are young and innocent, and have not been 'ruined' yet, you will perceive a group of dolphins. Yes, dolphins! Adults, on the other hand, perceive a couple in a suggestive embrace. If you are having trouble perceiving the dolphins, just reverse figure and ground. What normally constitutes the ground (dark areas), becomes a group of dolphins (the figures).

At a public exhibition at the University of Cambridge, it was tremendous fun to watch the adults and the very young children argue about the meaning of this image. Adults would exclaim to their children, 'What dolphins?' This image was also displayed in an illusion gallery at the Science Museum in Boston, MA. When asked if there was any controversy about displaying this image, they replied that once a group of nuns objected, but were quickly silenced when told that one's perception is based upon past experience. They giggled and went away. The Love of Dolphins is by Swiss artist Sandro Del Prete.

A Strange Flock

Actually, it is not a flock of sheep in the conventional sense, but a group of religious followers in a strange nudist cult.

Priming Illusion

Most people associate the word cow, white, and drinking, with milk and not water. By having the person repeat the word 'white', you are reinforcing the association.

It's a Matter of Counting

This is a wonderful priming illusion involving simple addition that will fool bank tellers and mathematicians. The correct answer is 4100, not 5000!

Hysteresis

The 'switch over' of interpretations tends to be at two different locations. Normally, you tend to lock into the first interpretation until there is overwhelming evidence to override it. This 'locking in' tendency is called hysteresis. This series of transforming images was originally devised by the English psychologist Gerald Fisher.

Stroop Effect

There are six words, and six colours to match. When the name and the ink colour are different, most people slow down. When you try to say the colour, you are also reading the word. The two different sources of information conflict, and it slows down your response time. This effect can also be applied to misnamed objects as well. It is not so much an illusion, as a perceptual confusion. It was discovered in 1935 by the Dutch psychologist John Ridley Stroop, and is known as the 'Stroop effect'.

*F*acial recognition is an extremely important part of the social behaviour of humans. We are able to recognize different individuals, their emotional expression or mood, veracity, intelligence, reliability, the comprehension of speech, as well as their gender and age. The ability to extract so much information from a person's facial expression requires a variety of perceptual tasks. Some perceptual tasks focus on specific facial features and ignore generalities. Other perceptual tasks may focus on generalities and ignore specifics. This is an incredible feat considering we are able to recognize literally thousands of faces, even though there are only generally minor variations on the basic facial pattern.

Facial recognition is 'special' in that it is processed very differently from object or scene recognition, and involves different areas of the brain. There is considerable evidence coming from studies of patients who have suffered damage to different parts of their brain, which has impaired certain perceptual functions. For example, patients who suffer from 'prosopagnosia' are unable to recognize familiar individuals by their faces alone. They are even unable to identify themselves when looking at their own reflection in a mirror.

Other evidence that the processing of faces is different comes from studies showing that upside-down faces are much harder to recognize than inverted objects. Interesting perceptual effects occur when certain areas of the face are inverted. Similar 'inversion effects' can be seen with stimuli other than faces, if the subjects are extremely knowledgeable at recognizing differences in their specific category. For example, dog breeders have their abilities to distinguish between breeds greatly diminished when pictures of dogs are presented upside-down.

The Cheshire Cat Illusion

This is a truly amazing illusion, but it requires two people to make it work! Have one person sit facing the mirror so that the white surface is on their right. Put the mirror edge against their nose so that the reflecting surface faces the wall. The other person should sit directly across from them. Position the first person so that their right eye sees just the reflection of the wall, while their left eye looks forward at the face of the person sitting directly across from them. You should see your friend's face on a level with yours. It is very important that they remain absolutely still and not move their head. Now the first person should move their hand in a circular fashion, using the attached blackboard eraser in front of the white surface. The face of the person that they are looking at will disappear except for their mouth and eyes – just like the Cheshire Cat in Alice in Wonderland!

One might need to try it several times, but don't give up, and allow some time to see the effect, as it is quite startling! The erasure can last for as long as five seconds if the eyes are kept stationary and there is no motion in the erased field of view. If the eyes move, the missing scene immediately reappears. If they follow the moving object, erasure does not occur.

 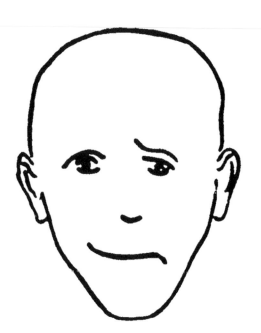

Who is Happier?

Which face appears happier?

The Inverted Head Illusion

This image of actor Jonathan Frakes does not look too scary, until you turn the picture upside down.

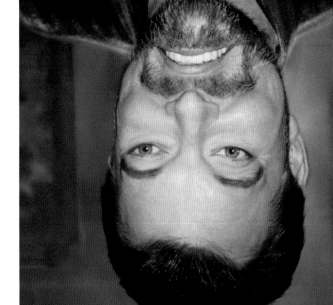

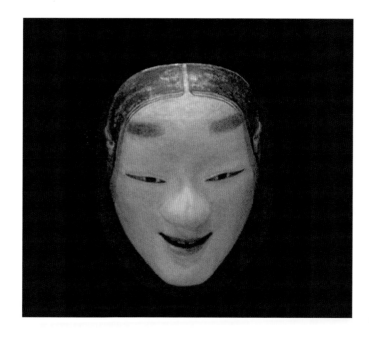

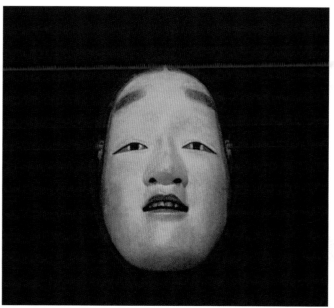

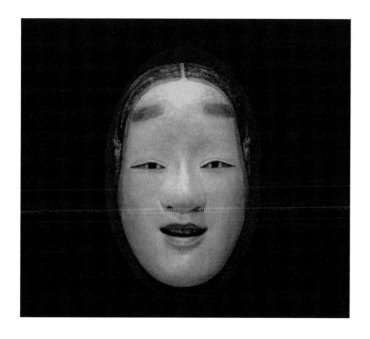

The Magical Mask of Noh

Compare the facial expression of the three masks.
Do they appear to have different expressions?
They are all the same rigid mask, but presented at
different angles.

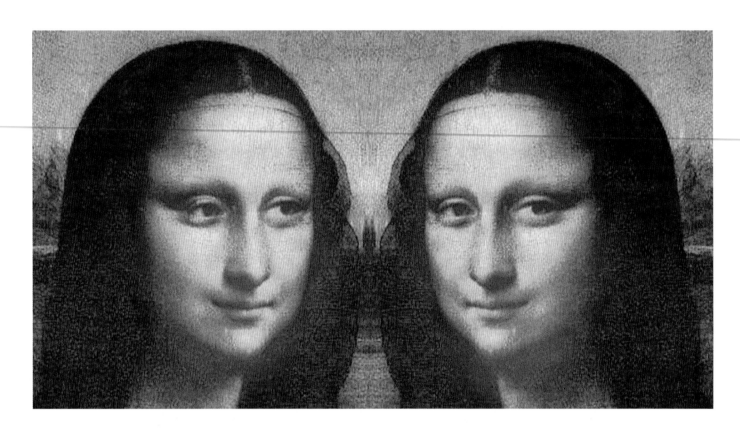

The Perceived Gaze Illusion

Which Mona Lisa is looking at you? Does the direction of gaze in the two versions appear to be different?

The Presidential Illusion

Which politicians do you see here? Take a closer look. Are you sure you're right?

Spatial Frequency Facial Effect

If you squint, blink, or defocus while looking at the pictures, the former English Prime Minister Margaret Thatcher should substitute for English Prime Minister Tony Blair. If this does not work, step back until your percepts change.

The Cheshire Cat Illusion

The image that you see is actually the combination of different images, which are fused in your brain; you notice your friend's face because it is more interesting than the white wall. When you move your hand, your visual system replaces portions of your friend's face with white, because the motion of your hand suddenly draws more attention to the white wall; however, since facial expression and gaze is also important, these areas remain while the rest of the face disappears.

Sally Duensing of the Exploratorium, an excellent hands-on museum, discovered the Cheshire Cat Illusion.

Who is Happier?

Many people see the right face as happier, even though the faces are almost mirror-images. The facial expression of the left face has a greater impact on our interpretation of a person's emotion. There is some controversy as to whether this asymmetry stems from the fact that the right hemisphere of the brain is more dominant in the processing of facial expressions.

The Inverted Head Illusion

A face that has its eyes and mouth inverted appears grotesque when it is upright, but not when it is inverted.

We have special areas of our brain devoted to processing faces, including their identity, emotion, gender, and direction of eye gaze. 'Configural' processing is important for face recognition, rather than recognition being based solely on the details of a face's constituent features. Because our experience with faces is almost exclusively with upright faces, these brain areas have become specialized for processing only upright faces. In particular, we are inefficient at interpreting the emotions of inverted faces. Because the face is initially upside down (only the mouth and the eyes are inverted), this facial area is inactive. When you turn the face right side up, you see the extreme nature of the expression.

It has been demonstrated that some species of monkeys, which hang from trees, and routinely see upside down faces, do not have this facial inversion effect.

This illusion was discovered by English vision scientist Peter Thompson, and was first used on an image of former English Prime Minister Margaret Thatcher, which is why it was formerly known as the Margaret Thatcher illusion.

The Magical Mask of Noh

The shape of the mask emphasizes certain features, particularly the contours of the mouth. Slight changes in viewpoint will change the relative position of the corners of the mouth to the lips. Our visual system is particular sensitive to tiny changes in facial features, and thus interprets the mask as having different emotional expressions.

The Perceived Gaze Illusion

There are at least two components to how we determine the direction of gaze. The first is the location of the eye in the eye socket and the second is the direction in which the head is pointed. We normally combine these two sources to determine the direction of gaze. In this case, we have an illusion, because mirroring the image on the right – except for the eyes, which remain unchanged (not reversed) – created the image on the left. This causes a dramatic change in the perceived direction of her gaze. Harvard vision scientist Shinki Ando created this Mona Lisa gaze illusion. W. H. Wollaston first noticed this effect in 1824.

The Presidental Illusion

Look closely at this image and you will see that it is not former President Bill Clinton and Vice President Al Gore. Although Clinton is depicted properly in the foreground, the background figure has Clinton's face, but with Al Gore's hair and trademark black suit. This shows how important context can be in forming your perception of a scene, and how seemingly important details can be inadvertently missed. In addition, hairline and width of the head are important to facial recognition. This illusion works best with people who are quite familiar with the Clinton/Gore team. MIT vision scientist Pawan Sinha created the Presidential illusion.

Spatial Frequency Facial Effect

The image of Margaret Thatcher is created using low spatial frequencies, and that of Tony Blair using high spatial frequencies. Quite different perceptual processes mediate the perception of expression, age and sex, as well as the recognition of a particular individual's identity. It has been suggested by some researchers that feature and surface details as represented by high spatial frequencies may be useful for some tasks, such as identifying a face. Low spatial frequencies may relate to configurational information and may be more useful for other tasks, such as identifying gender. When you squint, blink, or look at this image from a distance, you change the spatial frequencies.

The Thatcher-Blair illusion was discovered and reported by English vision scientists Vicky Bruce and Andrew Young in 1998.

Our visual/perceptual system normally assumes it is viewing objects from a 'generic' point of view, unless it receives evidence to the contrary. This means that a shift in position will not change the overall topology of a figure in a surprising way. The generic view principle is directly related to our perception of shape constancy or the tendency of the visual/perceptual system to perceive an object consistently through a variety of rotations and occlusions.

Included in this chapter are some of the most dramatic examples of illusions that exploit shape ambiguity and constancy. Here you will see examples where alignments have been deliberately or accidentally created to produce a misleading perception of an object's true shape. Nature is not normally devious and does not create objects that deliberately conceal gaps and obtrusions. Most accidental alignments in nature are broken either through movement of the object or the viewer, so they have little consequence in real life.

Audience responses to illusions revealed through motion are generally much stronger than responses to many other types of surprising illusions, suggesting that something very fundamental is going on when shape constancy is violated. Although these examples are presented on the page and therefore static, I hope you will get some idea of their impact.

A Two-Bodied Woman

To which body does the head belong in this unretouched photograph of the former First Lady, Lady Bird Johnson?

The Headless Horsewoman
Is this woman horsing around or what?

Piano

If you look in the mirror to the left you will see the reflection of a piano. If you look to the right, you will see a strange construction made out of piano parts, which cast the reflection of the perfect piano in the mirror.

Strange Cubes

The cubes on the outside of the building appear convex in the photograph above. If you look at the cubes from the side, you will see that they are really concave.

The Crazy Crate of Jerry Andrus

What is wrong with this crazy crate? Carefully examine the vertical limbs. Is the construction of this crate possible? Try to think about how this crate was constructed before looking below and seeing the answer.

The Crazy Crate Revealed

An Impossible Reflection

This triangle is possible in the mirror, but impossible as seen outside the mirror. How can that be?

A Strange Twist

Here is another example of a physically impossible triangle. If you look at the photo on the right, you will see its true construction.

Nob's Impossible Ledge

This is another example of an impossible object that works from only one point of view. Follow the ledge. The boy figure is sitting on top of the ledge, but where is the girl sitting in relation to the ledge? Does this physical construction make sense?

A

Moretti's Impossible Transforming Blocks

Photo A: From this angle, you will see three vertically aligned blocks at the top, which somehow merge into two vertically aligned blocks on the bottom. You are able to look through the sculpture to see the blue background.

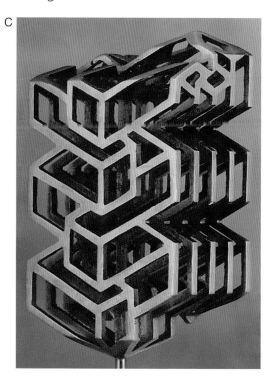

C

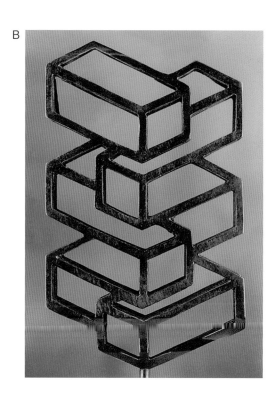

B

Photo B: Turn the sculpture clockwise by 90°. You will see a set of several horizontally aligned impossible blocks, and you can also look through the sculpture to see the blue background.

Photo C: The third view shows the sculpture from an angle midway between the other two angles. Italian artist Guido Moretti created this remarkable impossible transforming sculpture.

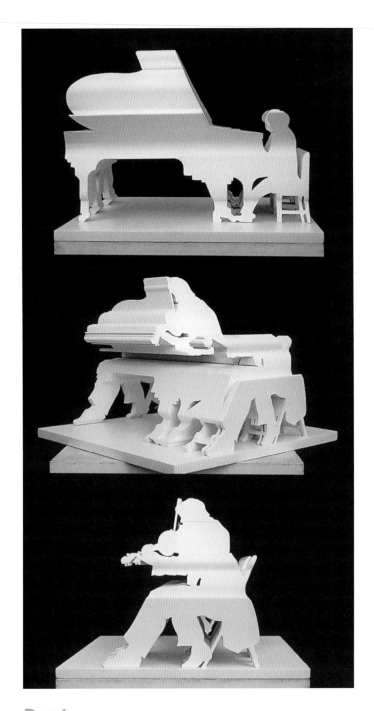

Duet

From one angle, the sculpture seen is of a pianist. If you turn the sculpture by 90° you will see a violinist. The middle photo shows an intermediate point of view, where you can see how the pianist transforms into the violinist.

194

THERE'S AN ANGLE TO THIS
What's going on?

A Two-Bodied Woman

The head belongs to the body on the right. Normally, there are no perceptual differences between men and women. However, this is one of the few examples of an illusion where Western women traditionally do better than men in matching the head to the proper body. In this particular case, women pick up on fashion cues, such as matching the hat with the proper dress.

Piano

The reflection of a perfect piano in the mirror only works when you look into the mirror from one very well defined viewpoint. Only at this angle will the pieces on the right subtend the same visual angle on the retina as a perfectly constructed piano, and so that is what you see. When you look to the right, you see the construction from a different visual angle, and its true construction is revealed. This shows in a very dramatic way that an infinite variety of shapes can give rise to the same retinal image. Japanese illusion artist Shigeo Fukuda created this dramatic distorted piano.

Strange Cubes

The insides of the cubes have been painted to look like the outside of the cubes. Given certain lighting conditions, it can be ambiguous for your visual system to determine whether something is either concave or convex. Again, you have a situation where the visual angle of the concave cubes will match that of the convex cubes. Moving to an extreme side angle will cause the structural cues to override the lighting cues, and the convexity is revealed. There is another interesting illusion associated with these cubes: they will appear to follow you as you move past them, even though they are stationary. This illusion has been popularized with inside-out masks, which when illuminated from behind, will follow the viewer in any direction as they walk past. This apparent movement is caused by a reversal in motion parallax. Motion parallax is what you encounter whenever you move past an object that has differing distances. You encounter motion parallax every time you look out of the side window of a moving car. Objects in the background tend to move relatively slowly compared to objects in the foreground. Also, the

objects move in a direction opposite to your direction of travel. In these reversed perspective illusions that also involve a structure with differing distances, what is physically the most distant part of the object is perceived as the closest part of the object and the physically closest part of the object is conversely perceived as the furthest part of the object. This perceptual reversal in perspective causes a reversal in perceived motion parallax, so that the object tends to move in the same direction as your direction of travel, which is a very weird sensation.

The man standing next to the cubes is the American magician James 'The Amazing' Randi.

The Crazy Crate Revealed

Here the Crazy Crate's true construction is revealed. The Crazy Crate originally appeared in a 1981 Omni magazine article about the original illusions of magician Jerry Andrus. Readers were challenged to figure out how Andrus constructed his crate; however, only about a third of the readers who wrote in with their answers came up with the correct solution. Of course, there are an endless variety of ways to construct such an impossible crate. There is a long tradition of constructing impossible objects in this way, which suggests an impossible construction when seen from one specific viewing angle.

An Impossible Reflection

The true construction of the triangle is revealed in the mirror. Even when presented with the correct construction of the triangle as seen in the mirror, your brain will not reject its seemingly impossible construction when seen outside the mirror. Bruno Ernst, who did much to popularize impossible figures and objects, constructed this impossible triangle.

A Strange Twist

Here, we have an example of an object where the visual angle of the curved lines has an identical projection on to your retina as straight lines. Remember that straight lines can be projected on to the retina from an endless variety of configurations, including curved lines, which at a specific angle appear to be straight. Unless

there is overriding evidence to the contrary, your visual system assumes that straight lines on the retina are projected from physically straight lines. When you move around this object, you get a real sense of surprise, because it does not transform in accordance with your experience of shape constancy.

Nob's Impossible Ledge

Japanese puzzle inventor Nob Yoshigahara created this wonderful impossible ledge. Like all of these impossible constructions, it only works from one special viewing angle.

Moretti's Impossible Transforming Blocks

Moretti's impossible blocks, aside from their seemingly paradoxical structure, provide another sense of surprise to the viewer. They violate one's expectations about shape constancy, which is the tendency of your perceptual system to keep consistent the true shape of objects as you view them from different angles. Experience dictates your expectation on how an object should transform as you move around it. If you look at photo A, you see a set of vertically aligned transparent blocks. The lines carefully occlude the structure seen in photo B. We normally don't encounter such 'devious' structures in nature, which is why photos A and B are considered 'non-generic' points of view. Moretti's blocks, because of this occlusion, transform in a very radical way – a vertical alignment transforming to a horizontal alignment. Swedish artist Oscar Reutersvärd's original impossible graphic designs served as an inspiration for this sculpture.

Duet

This sculpture consists of two silhouettes (the pianist and the violinist) at 90° angles to each other. In fact, you can create an endless variety of these types of silhouette sculptures by just carefully cutting a block from two different silhouettes at 90° angles to each other. There have also been examples made that incorporate three silhouettes, where the third silhouette is on the top surface. The noted Japanese artist Shigeo Fukuda created this wonderful example in 1976, which he called 'Encore'.

We live in an upright world, and we see the world as upright, even though the image that hits the retina is not only upside down but reversed left to right. Tilt your head and the world remains stable. Your visual system is very adept at correcting for head tilt, eye movements, and so forth. It provides you with a stable and upright view of the world. However, tilting your head and tilting an image are not the same thing.

In this chapter, we look at some amusing examples of images that contain secondary interpretations depending upon the orientation of the image. Some of these images acquire a new meaning when inverted and others when only slightly rotated. In this regard, faces have been the most popular subject for inverted figures.

No one knows when inverted images were first created, but they started to become popular on coins during the Reformation. These early types of topsy-turvy images typically contained hidden political and theological statements. In the nineteenth century, they took on a more amusing motif and were very popular in advertisements and puzzle cards.

In 1948, the artist Rex Whistler brought topsy turvy portraits to new heights in a book entitled OHO! The book had no front or back or rather two of each. Over the years, numerous artists and cartoonists have created books with inverted images, most of them directed at children.

A Flip Side of the Coin

It is not known who created the first topsy-turvy image, but they seem to have first appeared as political or theological statements on coins during the Reformation of the sixteenth century. This coin from some time after 1530 is the earliest example that I know. It depicts an image of the then current Pope which, when inverted, turns into the Devil. These coins were quite popular during the sixteenth century.

The Vegetable Gardener

Do you see a bowl of vegetables or a man's face?

Some French Heads

This is an example of some French invertible portraits of the early nineteenth century.

Courtship and matrimony

This was a harsh statement made on the institution of marriage that circulated in the United Kingdom in the latter part of the nineteenth century. The women are happy during 'courtship', but unhappy during 'marriage'.

THE INVISIBLE JOCKEY.

The Lost Jockey

The jockey seems to have fallen off his horse. Can you find him? This image
appeared on a puzzle card in 1888.

Captain of the Ship

The crew seems to have lost the captain. Can you find him?

Policeman

If you turn this policeman upside-down, he will be quite surprised.
This portrait is by Rex Whistler.

Little Lady Lovekins and Old Man Muffaroo

This is a single frame from a series of topsy-turvy children's cartoons published in the 1903 New York Herald by Gustave Verbeek. The New York Herald published Verbeek's sixty topsy-turvy stories every Sunday over a two-year period. Some of his stories involved the characters of Little Lady Lovekins and Old Man Muffaroo – when inverted, the characters would transform into each other.

Glee Turns Glum

Une moment they are happy and ın another moment they are sad. You can switch their mood by inverting the image. Roger Shepard created 'Glee Turns Glum'.

Jastrow's Duck/Rabbit Illusion

This is one of the most famous and classic of all illusions, which was created by the American psychologist Joseph Jastrow in 1888. Depending upon how you view the image, you can perceive either a rabbit or a duck.

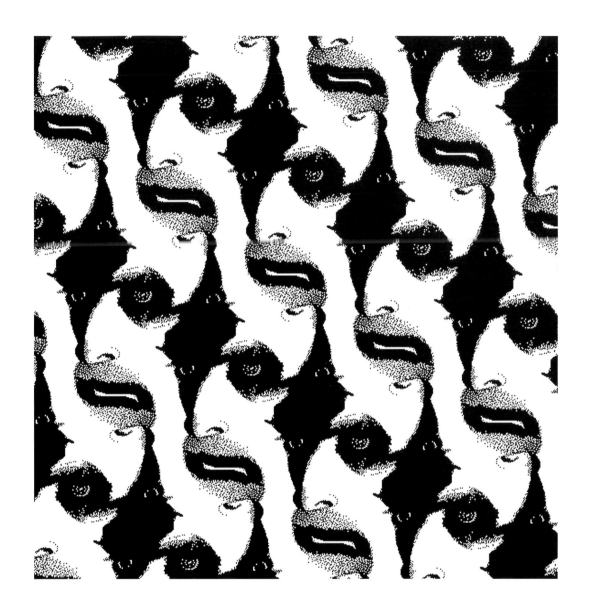

Homage to M.C. Escher

This image contains multiple tessellating portraits of Dutch graphic artist M.C. Escher. Turn the picture upside down and it still works. American artist Ken Landry created this tessellating topsy-turvy homage to Escher. Escher was famous for creating tessellating images.

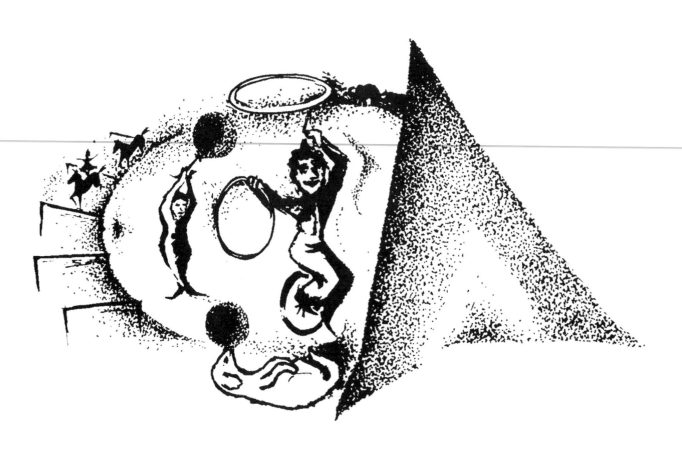

The Clown is Missing

Can you find the clown in this figure by Larry Kettlekamp?

A Flip Side of the Coin

It is not known who created the first topsy-turvy image, but they seem to have first appeared as political or theological statements on coins during the Reformation of the sixteenth century. This coin from some time after 1530 is the earliest example that I know. It depicts an image of the then current Pope which, when inverted, turns into the Devil. These coins were quite popular during the sixteenth century.

The Vegetable Gardener

Turn the image upside-down to see the portrait. Sixteenth century Italian artist Giuseppe Arcimboldo was famous for creating portraits out of strange objects. Several examples can be seen in the chapter on embedded images. 'The Vegetable Gardener' was painted by Arcimboldo in 1590.

Some French Heads

This is an example of some French invertible portraits of the early nineteenth century.

The Lost Jockey

Rotate this figure clockwise by 90°.

Captain of the Ship

Rotate this figure clockwise by 90°. This image appeared on a puzzle card in 1888.

The Clown is Missing

Rotate this figure counter-clockwise by 90°.

17 COMPOSITE IMAGES

Composite images consist of taking disparate smaller images and using them to form a discrete main image. The sixteenth century Italian artist Giuseppe Arcimboldi was famous in his day for creating portraits of famous people composed of fruits, vegetables, flowers, animals, and fish Arcimboldi influenced scores of imitators, even as recently as the twentieth century, including the great Spanish surrealist artist Salvadore Dalí.

In more recent times, a number of artists have also taken this concept to new levels. In the mid 1970s, the noted Japanese artist Shigeo Fukuda recreated Leonardo da Vinci's Mona Lisa out of many small versions of the same image. This was a laborious process, and while it worked the result was not entirely satisfactory. The Mona Lisa is the most popular iconic image to be recreated utilizing smaller objects, ranging from postage stamps to slices of burnt toast.

A more interesting approach was devised by the American artist Ken Knowlton, who created portraits out of disparate unretouched objects; an example is a portrait of the famous oceanographer and explorer Jacques Cousteau that Knowlton made out of seashells. More recently various computer scientists and programmers have developed methods to eliminate most, but not all, of the painstaking work that goes into creating artwork of this type.

A Hidden Portrait in a Still Life of Vegetables

Do you perceive a face or a collection of fruit?

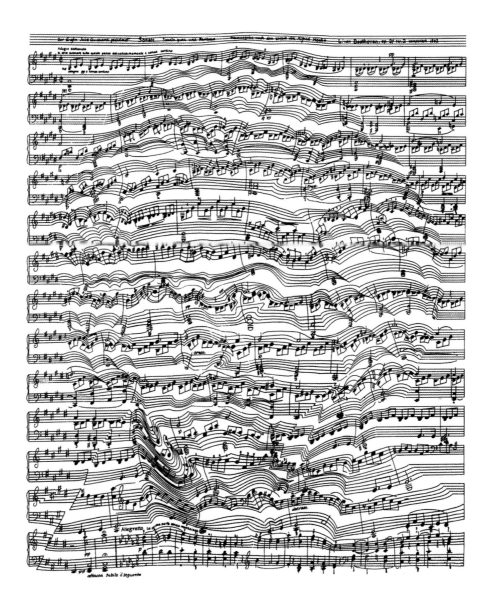

A Hidden Portrait of Beethoven in the 'Moonlight Sonata'

Can you recognize this portrait?

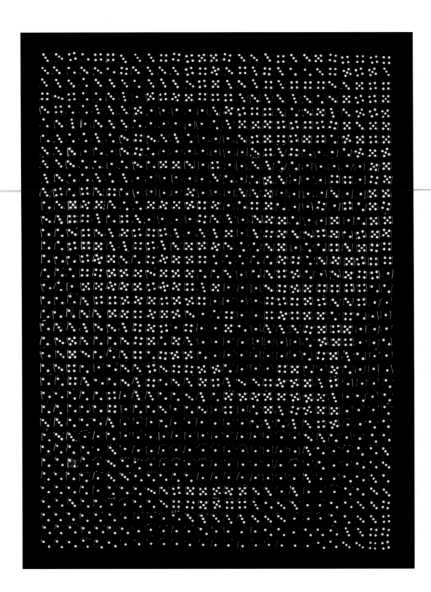

God Does Not Play Dice

Can you recognize the portrait?

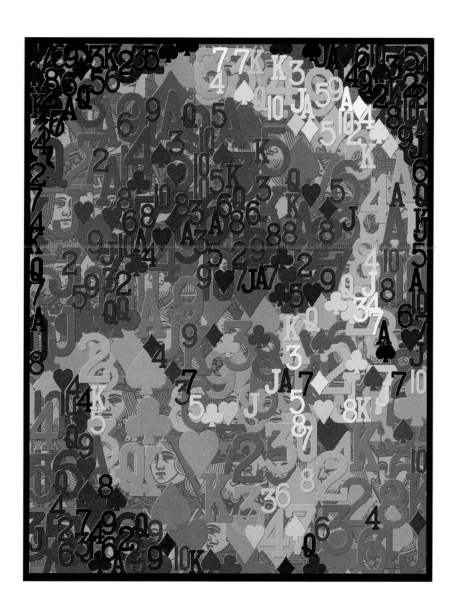

Lennart Greene

Stand back from this image and you will see a man's face made out of symbols from a playing card deck.

Basset Hound

If you look closely at this basset hound, you will see that it is composed of little animal photographs.

Buzz

This famous image of Buzz Aldrin on the moon is made entirely out of space and astronaut images. The sophistication of the artist comes out in the detail of the reflection on the helmet. If you view this image from a distance it will be remarkably well defined.

A Hidden Portrait in a Still Life of Vegetables

This is Giuseppe Arcimboldo's portrait of the Emperor Rudolph II.

Although you probably have no difficulty discerning the portrait in this collection of fruit, there are people who have suffered a stroke to a specific area of the brain, which codes for faces. This condition, known as visual agnosia, inhibits their ability to recognize faces and facial expressions. When shown a typical portrait by Arcimboldo, such as the one depicted here, they only see the collection of fruit, and are unable to discern the face. Other forms of visual agnosia inhibit the ability to recognize objects. In this case, they only see the collection of fruit and cannot discern the portrait.

A Hidden Portrait of Beethoven in the 'Moonlight Sonata'

This is a lovely example of creating a portrait of Ludwig van Beethoven from the opening movement of his famous 'Moonlight Sonata'. Thomas Bayle created this portrait in 1971.

God Does Not Play Dice

It is Albert Einstein, who once remarked, 'God does not play dice with the universe'. American artist Ken Knowlton constructed this portrait using only retouched dice. The dice are tilted in both the horizontal and depth planes.

Lennart Greene

This is Ken Knowlton's portrait of Lennart Greene, the world's best close-up card magician. In this case, the card symbols overlap. In contrast to Ken Knowlton's handcrafted portraits, this one was created utilizing his own specially developed computer software.

Basset Hound

This example was created by a computer which analyzes a target image, in this case the basset hound, in terms of several hundred values, which include among other things, edges, luminance, colour, etc. The computer then searches through a large database of stored images, which it has already evaluated in terms of the same variables. The computer then continues with a matching process that selects the best smaller image in terms of relative values for each region of the target picture. If the database of pictures is sufficiently large (for example, over ten thousand different images were searched for this picture) then the computer has a pretty good chance of finding a good match for each region. However, an artist still has to step in after the computer has done its selection process to 'tweak' the final result in those areas of the image that are most meaningful, such as those that relate to the eyes or the expression of the basset hound.

18 ANAMORPHOSES and TROMP L'OEIL

namorphic art is the process of greatly distorting an image only to have it revealed either from a single vantage point or from its reflection on a mirrored surface. A cylindrical mirror is the most common form, but cones and pyramids have also been used. The surprising appearance of the undistorted reflection or image is almost always met with wonder and delight.

It was Leonardo da Vinci who first experimented with anamorphic perspective. During the Renaissance, painters experimenting with perspective made great advances and perfected the techniques of stretching and distorting images. Anamorphic images became extremely popular and were an ideal means of camouflaging dangerous political statements, heretical ideas, and even erotic images. In the nineteenth century, when colour printing became inexpensive, the technique flourished as a popular parlour game. In the twentieth century, the Spanish surrealist Salvador Dalí created a series of anamorphic images and brought the technique to a new level. He distorted an image so that it would have a completely different interpretation from the hidden one seen reflected in the mirror.

Oblique anamorphosis is closely related to an artistic technique called trompe l'oeil (or 'deceiving the eye'). Both use perspective constructions to create a 'trick' image, but the difference lies in the nature of the trick. For an anamorphosis, the viewer is presented with something that does not make sense when viewed conventionally, and so he or she must seek out the unconventional viewpoint from which the trick is resolved. For trompe l'oeil, the viewer, standing in one particular place, is tricked into seeing an invented image as if it were reality. The idea is to create a flat surface that is as realistically three-dimensional as possible.

Leonardo's Eye

This anamorphic drawing made in 1485 by Leonardo da Vinci is the earliest known example of an anamorphosis. Although there are no notes accompanying this drawing, he does refer to the mechanics of anamorphic drawing in his treatise on painting, which is the earliest known reference to anamorphic perspective.

Holbein's Mysterious Skull

There is a skull hidden here. Can you find it and see it in an undistorted way?

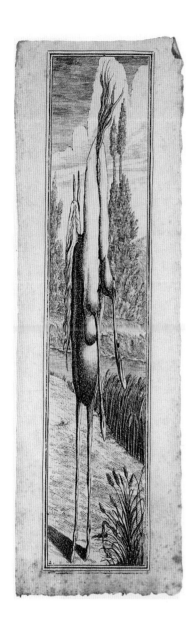

Into the Final Stretch

Tilt the book so that it is perpendicular to your face and, holding the book just below your eye, the horse should no longer appear distorted. This is an example of an early eighteenth century anamorphic drawing.

Stretching One's Mind

Tilt the book so that it is perpendicular to your face and holding the book just below your eye, the faces should no longer appear distorted. This is an example of an eighteenth century anamorphic drawing.

Dalí Anamorphosis

In the image without the cylinder, you can see butterflies. Look at the reflection of this image in the cylinder and you will see the butterflies transform into horse and riders. Spanish surrealist Salvador Dalí created this anamorphosis.

The Mysteriously Appearing Portrait of Jules Verne

This is a shipwreck scene in the frozen North based on the novel The Mysterious Island *by the famous nineteenth century French science-fiction author Jules Verne. Can you find the portrait of author Jules Verne? You will have to look at the reflection on the cylinder when it is placed over the moon.*

Homer on the Beach

Here you can see the reflection of the bust of Homer in the cylindrical mirror. This anamorphosis is by Hungarian artist Istvan Orosz.

An Anamorphic Homage to Da Vinci

In this painting by Dutch artist Hans Hamngren, the square in the centre is blank. When a pyramid-shaped mirror is placed on the square and you look straight down on it (as shown), you see the portrait of Leonardo da Vinci, who created the first known anamorphic image.

An Anamorphic Homage to Dalí

This painting has a blank circle in the middle of it. Only when a cone-shaped mirror is placed on the circle and you look into the point of the cone (as shown) can you see a portrait of the Spanish surrealist painter Salvador Dalí. Dutch artist Hans Hamngren created this anamorphic homage.

An Anamorphic Homage to Van Gogh

On the far wall is the reflection on a hanging wall mirror of Van Gogh's famous painting of sunflowers. On the table is the anamorphically distorted three-dimensional sculpture of Van Gogh's famous print. Japanese artist Shigeo Fukuda created this anamorphic sculpture.

The Magnificent Dome of Saint Ignazio

This ceiling appears to rise majestically towards the heavens, but is actually completely flat.

Can You Play This Violin?

This violin appears quite real, but it is as flat as the door it is on. Even the indentations on the door are painted.

A Building with a Single View

A typical building in New York City, or is it?

ANAMORPHOSES and TROMP L'OEIL
What's going on?

Holbein's Mysterious Skull

The Ambassadors, painted by German artist Hans Holbein in 1533, is without a doubt the most famous example of an anamorphic painting. In the bottom portion of the painting there is a strange shape, which when seen from a certain angle, transforms into a skull. The painting was originally hung on a staircase so that the skull may have appeared from below left or down the stairs.

Although anamorphic images had been in use as 'tricks' since the time of Leonardo da Vinci, it was gifted painters like Holbein who not only popularized the technique, but used it in a more intellectual fashion.

Although numerous explanations have been offered about the symbolic presence of the skull, including that it is a play on the artist's name, which means 'hollow bone' in German, the reason for its inclusion is still unclear.

Interestingly, there was no record of this strange image as an anamorphosis until 1873 – over three centuries after the picture was painted.

The Mysteriously Appearing Portrait of Jules Verne

This is a wonderful example of an anamorphic print, where an image is hidden in the main image, only to be revealed from a specific angle or in a reflection. Here, Hungarian artist Istvan Orosz took the art form to a whole new level. Formerly, artists would make a straightforward distortion of an image, which would be revealed on an appropriately placed reflective cylinder. The image by itself would just look distorted. Orosz managed to hide the image cleverly in an overall scene, which could be meaningful without the cylinder.

How did he create this image? First, he created the portrait. Then he mapped it on to an anamorphic grid which corresponds in a one-to-one relationship with the reflection on the mirror. Then, he 'buried' the portrait image within a larger scene.

The Magnificent Dome of Saint Ignazio

There is no doubt that the high point of trompe l'oeil was achieved in the spectacular work of the seventeenth-century Italian artist Andrea Pozzo in the Church of Saint Ignazio in Rome. When the church was to be built, it was to have an enormous dome, but the neighbouring Dominican monks complained that the resulting dome would cut their library off from light. Commissioning Pozzo to create a painted dome on a flat surface solved the problem. Nevertheless, this clever solution was not without its problems. If you stand away from the correct viewpoint (and there are only two correct spots in a very large church), the illusion crumbles. Although many people at the time were amazed by the illusion, Pozzo was severely criticized by other architects who complained about the painted architecture's 'construction'. Pozzo replied that a friend of his would bear 'all damages and costs' should the dome ever fall down!

A Building with a Single View

If you compare the large photo with the photo inset, you will notice that one side of the building is almost entirely hand painted with the exception of two windowpanes. The artist is Richard Haas and he has entitled this work '112 Prince Street Façade'. Note the painted side includes open windows, pulled shades, and air conditioners (with shadows).

There are many natural illusions. If you know how to look for them, you can find them almost everywhere. Perhaps because of this ubiquity, they have attracted more than their fair share of comment and disagreement.

The rainbow and the apparition known as 'angel glory' are examples of natural illusions that have caused wonder and admiration as well as religious awe. The Moon illusion has provoked decades of scientific controversy. At the far extreme are illusions such as anti-gravity hills and the face on Mars which have created cottage industries of crackpot theories.

The Moon Illusion

The moon illusion is one of nature's most famous and most controversial illusions. The full moon, just over the horizon, appears to be roughly one and half times the size that it appears to be when it is high over the horizon. The actual angular size of the moon does not change between the two locations. This doctored picture represents the relative sizes of the horizon and zenith moon, as it would appear to an observer. Interestingly, it is an effect that can't be captured on film. It has to be seen naturally to be appreciated.

Nature's Most Beautiful Illusion

The rainbow is nature's most beautiful natural illusion. In this unaltered photograph, how did the photographer capture this image of a rainbow on top of the Greek Parthenon? Was it just a matter of luck, or was it something else?

Hope You Are Not Thirsty

Another famous natural illusion is the mirage, which gives the impression of a surface of water lying just above the ground.

An Uphill Battle Against Gravity

Is this uphill or downhill?

Antisolar Rays

How dramatically do the sun's rays actually radiate?

The Angel Glory

Who is the angel?

They're Following Me!

Many people have identified travelling stars that appear to follow their cars as an extra-terrestrial craft coming to Earth for colonization purposes or to capture them as sexual slaves. Are they really seeing aliens?

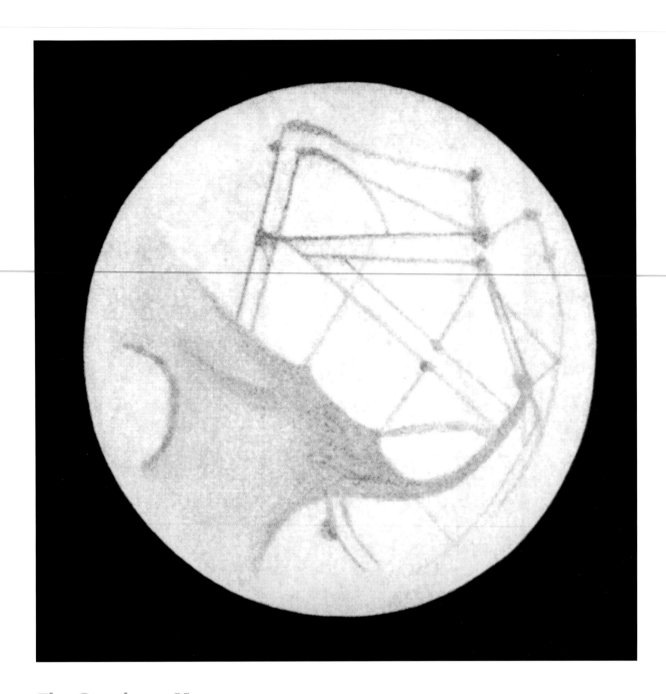

The Canals on Mars

This is an early map of the Martian surface by a distinguished American astronomer who claimed that these canals were evidence for the existence of intelligent life on Mars.

The Face on Mars

This NASA photograph of a Martian surface feature, which resembles a face, sparked a worldwide controversy over the possible discovery of intelligent life on Mars.

Climbing the Face of the Mountain

This photograph gives new meaning to the term 'climbing the face of the mountain'. This rock face is known as 'The Old Man on the Mountain', and was a famous tourist attraction located in New Hampshire, before it collapsed in 2003.

The Moon Illusion

The moon illusion has created quite a controversy about what gives rise to the effect, and there are many explanations for why the illusion occurs. The only general agreement seems to be that it is not an atmospheric effect.

Interestingly, the moon illusion is difficult to recreate in an unnatural setting. It does not work at all in a planetarium. Double exposures of the moon taken at both its horizon and zenith positions also destroy the illusion. Separate pictures of both positions also fail to capture the illusion. Therefore, it appears only to work in a natural environment. This is in contrast to many size/distance illusions, which can be reproduced photographically or by illustration.

Normally, when objects recede into the distance against a perspective background, not only does their visual angle get smaller, but they also approach a visual horizon. The moon, because of its enormous distance from us, does not change its visual angle much (only about two per cent) as it traverses across the heavens. However, your perception of its size does change. This is because your brain is interpreting the image on your retina based on visual cues, which it uses for assessing the size and distance of objects in proximity, i.e., between the visual horizon and you.

Nature's Most Beautiful Illusion

The photographer knew that there is no definite location for a rainbow, but only his position relative to the sun and the rain. The photographer positioned himself so that the rainbow would end exactly on the temple.

Hope You Are Not Thirsty

A mirage is produced by the refraction of light when it passes into a layer of warm air lying close to a heated ground surface, known as a temperature inversion.

In deserts, mirages may give the appearance of a lake or other large body of water in the distance; this is actually an image of the sky being refracted back up from the warm air lying over the sand. On tarmacked roads, mirages give the impression of puddles of water in the distance.

An Uphill Battle Against Gravity

This is a remarkable natural illusion that can be found all over the world, and many such areas have become tourist attractions where people watch the 'mysterious forces' at work that enable their cars to roll freely uphill. Of course, unscientific explanations and theories abound: regions of gravitational anomalies, ancient Indian burial sites, UFO landing sites, magnetic concentrations, and so forth. In truth, the effect, which is incredibly powerful, is a strong optical illusion caused by a misleading horizon line. It is the same illusion that is used in the anti-gravity tilted houses found in various tourist attractions, and discussed in the chapter on architectural illusions.

Antisolar Rays

The sun's rays are actually parallel. They look as if they converge due to perspective effects, in much the same way that train tracks appear to converge in the distance.

The Angel Glory

The Angel Glory, also known as the Brocken Spectre, is sometimes seen on mountaintops, when you are breaking through the mist with the clouds below. The apparition moves as you move and is clearly some magnified projection of yourself. A halo also appears around its head. No doubt, this illusion influenced many monks to believe that they had seen a divine apparition when scaling a mountaintop.

They're Following Me!

In fact, the 'travelling' star is not moving with you. It all has to do with motion parallax. Nearby objects move quickly past and further objects move slower. The moon and stars are so far away that their position hardly changes relative to your eyes. They, in fact, appear to be moving along with you. If you look at the moon, for example, out of your side car window, it will appear to be following you too.

The Canals on Mars

The existence of 'canals' or waterways on Mars was first reported in 1858 by the Italian astronomer Secchi, and it sparked a big debate in the scientific and religious communities on whether the canals were of intelligent origin.

All of these canals were just at the limit of visibility for naked eye astronomy, just where the brain starts to play tricks on vision. The canals were too faint for photography at that time. When we sent spacecraft to Mars, scientists expected to discover what the canals really were. Instead, they found that there were no canals, almost no straight lines at all. An occasional surface feature coincided with a canal or two, like parts of the Valles Marineris. Most of the canals did not exist at all, an amazing, contagious self-deception.

In the end, this optical illusion turned out to be a blessing. It prompted studies of all the planets in far more detail than had been done before and helped to fire the curiosity and launch the career of one of astronomy's most distinguished citizens.

The Face on Mars

A fairly substantial cottage industry has sprung up around the 'face on Mars' feature, with several books having been written about it, newsletters published, public presentations, press conferences, and, of course, 'supermarket tabloid' published reports. The basic premise is that the features are artificial, and are messages to us from alien beings.

There is no one in the established scientific community that takes this seriously, as these surface features are random, and due to our propensity to see faces in such patterns. Scientists figured it was just another Martian mesa, common enough around the Martian area of Cydonia where this photograph was taken, only this one had unusual shadows that made it look like a human head. When the site was re-photographed at a higher resolution on a subsequent mission, the facial features had all disappeared only to reveal an ordinary Martian land mesa, not unlike what is found in the American Midwest.

Illusions have been intentionally incorporated as architectural elements since antiquity, usually to achieve the desired effect of countering the effects of visual distortion. Throughout antiquity and into the Renaissance, there was much architectural experimentation using either 'counter-perspective' or 'accelerated perspective'. Counter-perspective is a device designed to counteract natural perspective – or how we view the world. Natural perspective occurs when, for example, a colonnade extends further away from the viewer; the columns appear to grow shorter and closer together as they approach the vanishing point. To create a counter-perspective illusion in such a case, the columns are spaced farther apart as they recede and their height increased so that from the given viewpoint (which must be controlled) they all appear to be the same height and distance apart.

The most famous example of architectural illusion is the crown jewel of ancient Greek architecture, the Parthenon, built in the fifth century BC – see opposite. Of course, obvious illusions have also been incorporated into architectural details to cause delight and surprise in visitors.

The Greatest Illusion of Antiquity

The Greek Parthenon is one of the greatest architectural wonders of the world, but it also incorporates an optical illusion to counter the visual distortion that would be present if the structure were actually built the way it is perceived.

The Greatest Illusion of the Renaissance

Giotto's magnificent bell tower, built in 1330 AD, adjacent to the Cathedral in Florence, gives the impression that all the floors and windows appear equally spaced, but in fact they are quite distorted.

A

B

A Magical Chinese Pool

Photo A: If you stand on the right side of the pool and look to the left, the pool appears to become increasingly shallower.

Photo B: If you stand on the opposite side of the pool, it now appears as if the left end of the pool is deep and becomes shallower to the right. This is the opposite of what you saw in the previous image. How is this possible?

The Saint Louis Arch

The famous Saint Louis Arch is a landmark monument that almost everyone recognizes, but what is not generally known is that it is not only an architectural feat, it is also an optical illusion. Can you tell what the illusion is?

Is This Balcony Safe?

If you look at the Futura Building in New York City from one side, the balconies appear to slant upward. If you look at this building from the other side, the same balconies appear to slope downward.

The Ames Room

Although the boy and the girl appear to be dramatically different in height, they are actually the same height. Additionally, although the room appears to be cubic, its true shape is quite different.

Off the Wall

In some popular tourist attractions, gravity appears to lose its grip, as people are able to lean off walls without falling, balls and water appear to roll and flow uphill, and objects appear to stand at strange angles without falling.

A Crazy Street

When people walk down a Crazy Street, they believe they are walking up, and vice versa.

Earthquake Damage?

Why would someone build tilted houses?

The Floating Cube

Is this cube floating in mid air?